HERE'S
THE DEAL
DON'T
TOUCH ME

HERE'S THE DEAL DON'T TOUCH ME

HOWIE MANDEL

WITH JOSH YOUNG

BANTAM BOOKS TRADE PAPERBACKS / NEW YORK

2010 Bantam Books Trade Paperback Edition

Copyright © 2009 by Alevy Productions, Inc.

Published in the United States by Bantam Books,
an imprint of The Random House Publishing Group,
a division of Random House, Inc., New York.

BANTAM BOOKS and the rooster colophon are
registered trademarks of Random House, Inc.

Originally published in hardcover in the United States by
Bantam Books, an imprint of The Random House Publishing
Group, a division of Random House, Inc., in 2009.

Photo credits can be found on page 221.

Library of Congress Cataloging-in-Publication Data

Mandel, Howie.
Here's the deal : don't touch me / Howie Mandel with Josh Young.
p. cm.
ISBN 978-0-553-38665-3
eBook ISBN 978-0-55380-786-8
1. Mandel, Howie. 2. Comedians—United States—Biography.
3. Actors—United States—Biography. 4. Television personalities—
United States—Biography. 5. Obsessive-compulsive disorder—
Patients—United States—Biography. I. Young, Josh. II. Title.
PN2287.M265A3 2009
792. 702'8092—dc22
[B]   2009034572

Printed in the United States of America

www.bantamdell.com

Book design by Susan Turner

I'd like to dedicate this book to
Terry, Jackie, Alex, Riley, Al, Evy, and Steve . . . the Mandels.

CONTENTS

IN COMEDY NOBODY CAN HEAR YOU SCREAM

I was devastated. I was humiliated. And I was probably finished, both professionally and personally. Those thoughts were racing around my head just minutes after doing Howard Stern's radio show.

This is not a joke, nor did it feel funny.

It was sometime in the late 1990s, and I was in the middle of a national press tour. Either I was promoting my dream come true, a nationally syndicated daytime talk show, *The Howie Mandel Show,* or it might have been right on the heels of its cancellation, when I wanted people to know I was still out there, hopefully funny, and available for work. I can't remember the date or exactly what happened, but I will never forget my feelings.

I had been in the business for twenty years as a stand-up comedian, actor, and now host, so I pretty much knew what to expect from these interviews. Most people ask the same softball questions.

But Howard Stern is a different animal. His show is about entertainment and controversy, sometimes at the expense of his guests. Even Steven Spielberg might have to sit between two midgets and a hooker and participate in Howard's circus while he's trying to plug his Holocaust movie. You must bring your A-game and be prepared to roll with whatever is thrown your way.

Howard Stern's setup is unlike any other. Normally, you just sit face-to-face with the host and answer questions and focus on being informative and entertaining. But on Howard's show, anyone can chime in at any time from anyplace in the room. Robin, a lovely young lady who has been his sidekick since he started in radio, sits in a glass booth off to the side. Fred, a longtime staple of Stern's show, usually sits someplace behind you. At that time, Jackie the Joke Man, who either provided comedic input verbally or passed along material to Howard, was also there. This was the regular irregularity of this show. Now add to this a guest whose name I cannot remember. I would have preferred two midgets and a hooker, because this interview would prove to be far more dangerous. It was tough enough as it was because of Howard's setup.

The mystery guest was wearing a T-shirt and loosely fitting sweatpants. Howard was playing a game where listeners had to guess this guest's special talent. I immediately became a radio show contestant, and I too had to join the guessing game. Being able to see him wasn't an advantage.

After many, many calls and repeated clues from Howard, nobody had guessed correctly. Finally, Howard revealed this guy's special talent. The man stood up, loosened his sweatpants, and dropped them to his knees. It was like going to a show where the curtain is dropped and the main attraction is revealed. He had a huge penis, the likes of which I have never seen.

I don't know how to describe what I saw. You hear of men with large penises. The best way to describe this was a large penis with a small man on the end.

With Howard calling the play-by-play, the guy began doing tricks with his member. He wrapped his penis around his leg clockwise and tied it into something of a knot. This guy was an amazing talent. I have no idea where he is today, but he's probably huge—not as far as success goes, but wherever he is, he's huge.

The whole event was so Howard. He presents the biggest, craziest penis ever seen—on radio.

I was awash with different emotions. The first was jealousy. That was followed quickly by discomfort. I'm not a homophobe, but there is nothing more disconcerting than a man sitting next to you playing with his penis. I was supposed to be there promoting myself, but I felt as though I were sitting on a two a.m. train back to Brooklyn—not that I've been on a two a.m. train to Brooklyn, nor would I expect the man next to me to be playing with his penis, but I don't have any other point of reference for this experience.

When the penis manipulator finished his tricks, Howard said goodbye. The guy zipped up and headed toward the door. As a little boy, I had been taught to wash my hands after going to the bathroom, even if I had touched nothing but my own penis. This guy I had been sitting next to didn't piss, but I promise you he touched his penis. Wait, I'm thinking, where are the hand wipes? As any person would, he grabbed the knob, pulled the door open, and was gone. He might have been gone, but in my mind, there was so much more of him still in the room than needed to be.

Now that he had left, it was my time to shine. My job would be to chime in from time to time with some witty repartee. That being said, I don't believe my repartee was witty, if even existent. My entire focus was on that doorknob that I knew I would have to handle.

As Howard went on, I felt like Charlie Brown in *Peanuts* when the teacher speaks and all Charlie hears is "Waw, waw, waw." All I could think about was how I was going to get through the door without touching the knob.

The next thing I seem to remember hearing is Howard thanking me for stopping by. In fact, if you listen to a tape of the broadcast, it may not be anything like this. I'm just telling you what was going on in my head.

After the goodbyes and thank-yous, I headed toward the door. When I reached the threshold, I very casually, and as naturally as I could, asked, "Can somebody open the door for me? I don't want to touch the knob because the guy had his penis all over his hands, and his hands touched the door." I didn't think it would be an issue.

But Howard wanted me to open the door myself.

I didn't want to. He had touched his penis and then he touched the doorknob.

This back-and-forth lasted through the commercial break, and soon we were back live on the air. Howard announced that Howie Mandel wouldn't touch the doorknob because it had penis residue on it, and the drama escalated.

I stood there for what seemed like an eternity. Though I wasn't physically trapped, I was mentally trapped. At this moment, nothing else existed for me but this problem. I had no awareness that this back-and-forth was being broadcast nationally. I was making no effort to be funny or entertaining. I just wanted to get out of that room, so I lifted the veil of funny and went to honesty.

I said something to the effect of: "The joke is over, I cannot touch this door. As much as I imagine this is entertaining, this is real. It's something that I cope with and talk to a therapist about. It's a real issue, and it's part of a bigger condition called OCD. Obsessive-compulsive disorder."

That admission was a major event in my life. The fact that I had told Howard Stern that I have a serious mental issue and see a therapist for it may not seem like anything to you, the reader, but this was a big hammer that landed for me. It was like revealing my darkest secret.

I remember feeling heart palpitations, a shortness of breath, and an anxiety attack coming on, which is why my memory of the story is somewhat clouded. I could not touch that doorknob. Truthfully, I don't know what Howard was saying. I do know that I told him what I was suffering from was real. I do know that I was panicked. I do know that I wasn't in the mode to entertain. And I do know that it didn't feel good.

As serious as all this was to me, I'm sure it meant nothing to him. I don't believe that anybody in the room felt they were witnessing something of great consequence. Even so, many times when I'm being serious like that, people don't realize that I am being serious. In comedy, nobody can hear you scream.

Finally, somebody opened the door and let me out of the studio. As the door closed behind me, a real sense of devastation came over me. If there is a palpable feeling to devastation, that was it. I had just told the world that I'm a nutcase.

My mind was racing. What are the consequences of talking about this? First and foremost, I said something that was personally embarrassing and would be embarrassing to my wife and children, who have no interest in being in the public eye, least of all as a relative to a mental case. Are people not going to hire me? Every show costs millions of dollars and employs hundreds of people. Why would the producers risk putting someone at the helm who has mental issues?

I know this sounds crazy—no pun intended—but you have to realize that I was born in 1955 in Toronto, Canada, and having mental health issues and going to a psychiatrist was not the norm. Society has always attached a stigma to mental health issues, and I'm very much a part of that culture. Outwardly, I seemed to be striving and functioning, but my mental health was not something I talked about publicly. It was certainly not something I talked about on a comedy radio show. If I was going to discuss such a serious subject, it would be with my family, my friends, or my therapist. And maybe if I talked about it publicly, I would do it eleven years later in a book. But not on *The Howard Stern Show.*

I was truly devastated. I walked down the hall, and it was very dark. It probably wasn't, but it felt dark. Then I got into the elevator. The door closed, and it was even darker. The elevator went down, which was such a great metaphor for how I was feeling. In my mind, everybody was calling everybody else and saying, "Did you hear Howard's show? Howie Mandel's a mental case." My kids were already being ridiculed. My wife was holed up in the house. At *USA Today*, they were stopping the presses. CNN had a breaking news flash. The world was coming to a halt to absorb this news.

I walked out of the elevator and through the front door onto the street into a teeming mass of humanity known as Manhattan. Even though I felt I was standing amidst millions of people, I had never felt more alone. My head was hung. I didn't want to make eye contact with anyone.

I heard a voice. I kept looking down at the sidewalk, and I saw a pair of feet in my periphery. A man's voice said, "You're Howie Mandel."

My heart sank. I thought, This is it. This is the precipice of devastation, and I'm about to go over it. Without looking up, I revealed shamefully, "Yep."

"I just heard you on *Howard*," he said excitedly.

"You did . . ."

"Are you really a germaphobe?"

This random guy on the streets of New York was about to

begin the public ridiculing that I had brought upon myself. "Yes," I mumbled.

"And you've got OCD . . . ," he continued.

And now I was descending closer to hell than I ever imagined. Running into traffic to get away from this guy was starting to look like the only option. "Yes, I do," I confided.

There was a long pause. And then came the two most dramatic words that I have ever heard. They were the words that changed my life and probably are the reason I am writing this book. He said, "Me too."

He walked away and left me standing with those two words in my head. That was the first time I realized that there was at least one other person who shared my pain. I've always had people around me who help me and take care of me, but they don't share in my personal misery. Nobody is inside my head. But there was one guy on the streets of Manhattan who shared what I'm feeling. I was not alone.

The walk out of Howard's studio, down that hall and into the elevator, and onto the streets of Manhattan was one of the darkest trips of my life, because I didn't know what I had done or what would happen next. But in the days, weeks, months, and years after that guy said, "Me too," I found there were countless others. People contacted me to tell me they have OCD and that they're working through it in therapy. They would ask me to tape a message to their son so he knew that he wasn't alone. They would thank me for talking about OCD publicly. As much comfort as I feel in knowing that I'm not alone, they took comfort in knowing that there is somebody else who suffers as they do.

Without knowing it, I had done myself a service. To date, I'm not aware that revealing my OCD or discussing it has ever cost me a job. OCD has cost me peace in my own head, which it does constantly. There's nothing I can do about that—though talking about it and writing about it is a deterrent from sitting quietly and letting myself sink into that hole.

It was the one moment when I publicly revealed the most intimate part of who I am. In this business, people always think they know you. In my career, this feeling has been fractured because my persona has always been so different. I've been the wacky guy who put the rubber glove on his head as a comedian. I've been the voice on *Bobby's World* to five-year-olds and their parents, who weren't the same people who knew me from comedy. I've been an upstart intern on *St. Elsewhere*, which was a highly acclaimed prime-time drama in the 1980s. I've been the empathetic game-show host on *Deal or No Deal* and the prankster on *Howie Do It*. But as big a fan as you might be of any of those personas, each one contains only a small piece of me. The closest to who I am each and every day is the person who couldn't escape from Howard Stern's studio.

HERE'S THE DEAL DON'T TOUCH ME

ONE

WELCOME TO ME

November 29, 1955. Toronto, Ontario, Canada. Mount Sinai Hospital. Howard Michael Mandel was born to Albert and Evelyn Mandel. I have absolutely no recollection of my infancy, but I'm told I was the happiest, most idyllic child, not to mention the cleanest child known to man.

As excited as my mother must have been about having me, she tells me that she felt like a child herself. She was just twenty-three, and my father was twenty-nine. She was really nervous about her baby boy and wanted to protect him from the evils of the world at that time—the Commies, nuclear proliferation, and, most important, the invasion of germs.

Whenever somebody came over to see her baby, God forbid they should touch little Howard's teeny fingers. As soon as they left, she would take me into the bathroom and scrub my hands with soap and water. If somebody sniffled and touched my crib, my mother would mark the spot in her mind. She would remember that it was two inches to the left of the headboard, and again, as soon as that person left the room, she would hit that spot with the Lysol, putting me back in my sterile environment.

You might think this was over the top, but the apple didn't fall far from the tree. The first and all recollections I have of visiting my grandparents on my mother's side were of approaching the house and seeing my "bubbie" outside the front door on her hands and knees, waxing the concrete veranda. Waxing. Concrete. Outside. There was no way she was going to allow anyone to track filth into her home. She believed that this was the first line of defense toward maintaining a safe environment—that is, if you ignored the fact that it was very easy to slip and break your neck before you rang the doorbell. Let's weigh the odds here: no dirt on your feet, or a broken neck. She seemed to lean in favor of no dirt on the feet.

Once you were inside, not much changed. As in many homes in the Northeast and Midwest, inside the door there was a tray where you could remove your boots so you didn't track mud and snow into the house. I know there was a boot tray, but my grandmother's was covered in newspaper, because God forbid the boots should touch the tray. In fact, I don't think I ever touched any of the furniture or carpets in her house because it was all covered with plastic. Everything was hermetically sealed in its place.

So when I now see a picture of me as an infant, posed on a chair in my living room and separated from that chair by a sheet of plastic, it seems to make some sense.

I started my life with the cleanest of slates, so to speak. Everything went swimmingly well for Howard for those first two and a half years in what was metaphorically a perfectly chlorinated pool. But then comes my first memory of infancy. I may not be accurately depicting the facts, but I promise you I'm accurately depicting my memory.

In the last week of October 1957, my mother disappeared. My dad went off to work during the day, driving a cab, and a strange woman showed up at the house to take care of me.

I think her name was Mrs. Weatherburn. I can't remember her name as accurately as I can remember the fact that she wore dentures. I didn't know what dentures were at the time, which made things worse. In addition to being terrorized by the fact that my mother was gone, I had to deal with an old woman who would go into our bathroom in the morning, put her fingers in her mouth, rip out all her teeth in one piece, brush them in front of me, and then put them back into her face.

I felt as if I were living in a horror movie. You have no idea how scared I was. Every day after my father went to work, I was left alone with a lady who ripped out her teeth. All I wanted was my mommy. But Mommy had gone away. I felt like a small, human Jewish Bambi. In the span of seven days, I went from gleefully happy to utterly miserable.

At the end of the week, my dad informed me that we were going to pick up "the baby." I remember this as clearly as yesterday. I can tell you honestly I had no idea what "the baby" meant. He seemed excited about "the baby." He could have said we were picking up a lemur. It would have meant the same thing to me.

I want to clarify what "the baby" was. In the fifties, when women were pregnant and ready to give birth, they checked into the hospital for a week. At that time, children were not welcome as visitors in the maternity ward, which is why I didn't see my mother for a week. All this makes sense to me now, but it didn't then.

We drove to Mount Sinai Hospital in downtown Toronto. I hadn't been there in almost two years, and I didn't recognize the place. It was a cold, gray, drizzly day. We parked in the back of the building, and my dad disappeared inside to get "the baby."

I was sitting quietly in the car with Mrs. Weatherburn, waiting. I remember not saying anything for fear that she might talk to me and bare her teeth. I was afraid that those teeth might jump out at me at any moment. After what seemed like an eternity, my mother emerged through the hospital's big metal door.

I remember watching my mom, who was my whole life, coming out to the car. I was so excited to see her again. She was carrying something wrapped in blankets. This must be "the baby." My dad helped her into the backseat. Mommy leaned over, said, "I love you," and gave me a kiss.

As she leaned over, I looked inside all those blankets she was carrying and I could see a little face. There was another person with my mommy. Who was this? Was it "the baby"?

From that moment on, my life was different. My mom

tells me that my whole demeanor changed. My sense of contentment was replaced with agitation.

Stevie—that's what they called "the baby"—needed very little attention. He had a couple of meals a day, a diaper change once in a while, and the rest of the time he slept. If you do the math, it worked out to about 5 percent of my mom's attention. I received the other 95 percent. It wasn't even fifty-fifty between the two brothers, but I was completely distraught. Up until then, it had been me, me, me, me, me, me, me, me. Now it was me, me, me, me, him, me, me, me. Can you understand how devastating this was for me?

Here are some of the ways I handled it. I would walk into the room where they kept little Stevie and scream as loud as I could to make him cry. Then my mom would come in and yell at me for waking up "the baby." But remember, she was yelling at *me*, so I had all the attention. One time he stuck his hand through the bars of his crib, and I pulled on it as hard as I could. He had to go to the hospital because I ripped his arm out of the socket. That was horrible, but again, I got a lot of attention for that.

I don't know how this is possible, but throughout our childhood, my brother always had—and continues to have—an amazing love for me. Whenever my mom got upset with me, she'd threaten: "That's it! Wednesday is garbage day. I'm throwing you out with the garbage." My brother would break into tears and plead, "Please don't throw Howie in the garbage." He was so scared that I would be tossed out and he wouldn't have me around. My punishments seemed to punish him more.

I now believe that my brother, Steve, is the reason I have become a performer today. From the moment "the baby" appeared, I spent every waking moment trying to get all the attention. Regardless of whether that attention was positive or negative, it was attention just the same. I didn't make the connection at the time, but child experts say that a good part of your personality and who you are going to be is formed in the first years of your life. If that is true, then the sick need that I have to be accepted and appreciated by people I don't know stemmed from spending my entire childhood trying to get 100 percent of the attention. Obviously, you can't get *all* the attention, but I promise you I'm still trying.

At age four, I was about to meet some other people vying for attention. I was enrolled in school. In the grade of kindergarten at Dublin Public School, to be exact. Looking back, I realize I didn't have a lot going for me. I was allergic to dairy products; I was suffering from seeping eczema and constant ear infections; and I was a bed wetter. And, oh, I forgot, a maniacal attention seeker.

I say bed wetter because I wet the bed, but wetting myself extended far beyond the bed. When I analyze this now—not that I or anyone was diagnosed at the time—I believe this wetting could have been a direct result of having attention deficit hyperactivity disorder, ADHD for short. I have been professionally diagnosed with this disorder as an adult. The characteristics of this are an inability to focus, impulsive behavior, and being easily distracted. I have come to realize these symp-

toms have plagued me throughout my life. I remember thinking as a child, I have to go to the potty, and then I would see
something shiny or hear a voice, and I would be off on a tan-
gent. Soon, I would realize that my pants were wet, and I
hadn't made it to the potty.

I don't want you to think I wasn't innovative. Here were
the remedies to keep the other kids from realizing that
Howard had just pissed himself: Through a varying array of
excuses, I would dismiss myself quietly before anybody noticed the wet spot covering the front of my pants, find my way
to a puddle or a ditch, and submerge myself. There were no
puddles or ditches right out the front door, so I had to travel a
far distance to trip and fall into a puddle. But this allowed me
to hold my head up high and declare proudly to my class-
mates, "I've fallen into yet another puddle!" Throughout my
early school years, I was known as the kid who would fall into
a puddle or ditch six or seven times a year. In retrospect, this
seems equally as embarrassing.

My kindergarten teachers were named Mrs. Smith and
Mrs. Judge, and I was called by my full name, Howard. I'm
Howie now because Howard makes me cringe. Howard comes
mostly with the connotation of anger. There was never any good
news after Howard. Nobody ever said, "Howard, we have something great for you." It was always a demand or a reprimand.

All I remember doing in kindergarten was arts and crafts.
Once we were doing a landscape, and three days in a row I apparently painted the sky purple. The teachers thought I was
trying to be funny or combative, so they made me stand behind the piano. This was my first sense of what it felt like to be

an outcast. All of the other kids were having fun painting skies, and I was placed behind the piano.

One day, my mom visited me at school and found me behind the piano. When it was explained to her what I had done, she asked me to show her the blue crayon. I picked up the purple crayon. She consulted with our family doctor about why I would do that. He eventually figured out that I was colorblind. Oh, good, let's add that to my list of attributes.

So I remember my kindergarten years as everybody playing while I stood behind the piano, not knowing why I was different from the other kids.

By first grade, I had other issues. Everyone including me knew how to tie their shoelaces. But when the other kids' laces came untied, they would retie them. When my laces touched the filthy ground, I could not bring myself to touch them. My grandmother had not waxed the schoolyard. The horror of touching those laces far outweighed the embarrassment of spending the rest of the school day and my trek home walking like Quasimodo, dragging my foot so that I wouldn't lose my shoe. It's amazing that nobody ever mentioned how strangely I walked.

To this day, my mother recounts a miserable child walking home from school. She could see me from our porch two blocks away, dragging one leg with the untied shoelace behind me.

My young brother, Stevie, had a sense of the things that horrified me. Like most brothers, we got into many scuffles. I'm not saying we didn't punch and hit and cause personal injury. But if I was chasing him, his last bastion of defense was running to the laundry hamper, removing the lid, and waving it in my direction. Just the sight of that lid was like my kryptonite. The tables would turn, and now he was chasing me. I would scream as if someone were after me with a knife. The lid of the laundry hamper doesn't sound toxic, and I don't know what I thought would happen if it touched me, but I was horrified and the fight would come to an end. Everyone including me just accepted this as the norm.

Looking back, I see that I was accumulating many letters—ADHD and OCD. It would take decades to solve this puzzle. I'd like to buy a vowel, Pat.

I remember agitation being the pervasive emotion of my childhood. I believe this is a rough start for any child. I was a lactose-intolerant, color-blind outcast with ear infections who had a maniacal need to be the center of attention, sometimes walked like Quasimodo, randomly fell into puddles, and had a crazy fear of hamper lids. With all these gifts, I was off to make my way in the world.

As tough as this sounds, I lived a wonderful childhood. One of the biggest highlights was our family's yearly trip to Miami Beach during winter break. Remember I'm a Jew, so this was my Christmas. The night before the trip was like Christmas Eve. I had always heard about how all the non-Jewish kids couldn't wait to wake up on Christmas and open their presents. They would stay up late with anticipation and then get up before the sun rose on Christmas morning and sit under the tree with the presents until their parents woke up.

My parents would put my brother and me to bed early because we were leaving at four a.m. Steve and I had rooms across the hall from each other, and we would sleep with our doors open and try to stay awake all night. We could hear our parents in the living room watching Johnny Carson and smell the pizza they had ordered.

"Steve, we're going tomorrow," I whispered across the hall.

"This is great," he whispered back.

The next morning, our parents bundled us up in our winter coats and put us in the family car for the three-day journey to Miami. They lodged a suitcase between us so we wouldn't fight and gave each of us lame toys to play with as a distraction. One was a small game board of a man's face that was filled with little pieces of metal shavings you could move around with a magnetic pen to make a hairpiece or a mustache on the man. The other was a piece of cardboard that had a sheet of opaque plastic on top of carbon paper. You could draw a picture and then lift the plastic to make it disappear.

People are probably reading this, thinking, I had those games, they weren't lame, I loved them. So did I—for the first several hours. Let me go further: maybe even the first day. But for three eight-hour days, there are only so many faces and mustaches one can draw. And then let's not forget about my undiagnosed inability to focus.

The anticipation of getting to Miami was my salvation. We'd strip off layers of clothing as we got farther and farther south, until finally we were in Miami Beach. I remember coming over the causeway with my face pressed to the window and seeing streets lined with palm trees and brightly colored hotels lined up on the beach. It was like arriving in Oz.

We stayed in what is now known as South Beach, either at the DiLido (now the Ritz-Carlton), the Nautilus, or the Surfcomber, always in one room with three beds, one roll-out for my parents and one each for my brother and me. I would fall asleep and wake up when it was still dark out, and then I'd wait until the sun came in through the blinds. At the first little streak of light on the ceiling, I would get out of bed and crack the blinds. It felt like days before anyone else woke up. As usual, I was agitated, but I couldn't wait to get outside so I could be agitated in a sunny place.

On one particular trip, I was playing in the sand, which I loved. My favorite game was to dig holes near the ocean. I would dig and dig until I reached water, which caused the sides to cave in. Then I would dig faster and try to beat the sides from caving in. I don't know what I thought the endgame was, but I kept digging. I never met any Asian people, so apparently I didn't dig deep enough.

Sometime during my morning of digging, a sand fly landed on my leg and bit me. It wasn't a painful bite. I didn't even remember the bite, but I now know that I was bitten by a sand fly.

The next morning, I woke up with a little bump on my leg. It looked like a mosquito bite, so I scratched it. When I moved my hand away, the bump had elongated and moved a half inch from where it had been right in front of my eyes. I thought, This can't be possible.

By the end of the vacation, I had about twenty of these

bumps, which had grown to look like worms under my skin. I had one on my wrist and ten on each leg. They were itchy, and they moved. I was freaked out, and I sensed that my mom was, too, though she didn't show it.

Three days later, after driving across the United States, adding sweaters and coats as we moved farther north, we were back in Toronto.

Our first stop was Dr. Weinberg's office. I really liked Dr. Weinberg. He was a calming presence, but I knew that what I had was a big deal because the only doctor I had ever seen in my life sent us to another doctor. If Dr. Weinberg couldn't help me, then I must have monsters living in me. I was really scared.

The new doctor identified this condition as larvae being laid under my skin. Apparently, the sand fly laid its eggs in me, and they were being hatched just under the surface. We were informed not to worry because this happened frequently . . . *to cattle*! After some research, I was prescribed a pill that, to date, had been given only to a cow. My recollection is that the pill was the size of a DVD—and not a great-tasting DVD, I might add.

The next morning was not unlike any other. I got up, brushed my teeth, had breakfast, took my cow pill, and went to school. But about an hour into class, I passed out in front of everyone.

Shortly after that, I was sent to a third doctor, who I now know was a dermatologist. He touched my bites and watched them move. He seemed excited by what he was seeing and asked if we could come back in two days.

Apparently, there happened to be some sort of dermatology convention coming to Toronto. Dermatologists from all over the world gathered to learn and study cures to various illnesses. Lo and behold, this dermatologist had found me, and I was going to be the prime specimen to be exhibited at his symposium: "A Boy with the Disease of Cows."

After a couple of days, we showed up at the designated address. The dermatologist brought me into an examining room. He removed my pants and put me on the examining table. He began touching the bites on my legs, and the little monsters began moving under my skin.

The dermatologist excused himself and returned with four other doctors. Now there were five doctors standing over me, hemming and hawing at the movement under my skin. He then explained to his colleagues the necessary treatment.

At that point, I didn't really understand what he was saying, but I can now tell you as an adult that he suggested liquid nitrogen. For anybody who doesn't know, liquid nitrogen is similar to dry ice. It's incredibly cold, so cold that it actually burns.

He explained that a sand fly had laid its eggs and their larvae were living under my skin. Every time I scratched one, it would motor to a safe haven. I did have enough wherewithal at that age to understand that there was something living in me. There is nothing more terrifying than picturing something icky crawling around inside of you.

The doctors all moved in closer to see the results of this experiment. I wasn't given any painkiller, anesthesia, or comfort. In front of all these people, the dermatologist prepared to cure me of these monsters that inhabited my body.

The nurse brought in the liquid nitrogen. The dermatologist placed a drop on the ridge of the bump at the arch of my foot. As the drop hit the ridge, it actually sizzled and burned. I screamed. I was being burned alive in front of an audience. Not only did the bump sizzle, it bubbled and formed a giant blister.

I could see the flesh come off my leg and bubble up like a sphere. The pain was piercing. I was screaming and yelling. The doctor had the chance to hit only one or two before I looked desperately at my mother, who was crying, saying, "Please, stop!" Even the other doctors were telling him to stop.

That's one of the first palpable memories I have of not being in control. I don't know why I didn't get off the table and run. When I've told this story, people say, "You were only a kid." But being a kid almost gives you the excuse *not* to be in control. I don't remember struggling to get off the table. They didn't have to hold me down. I acquiesced to that horror I had to endure.

My mother ended the liquid nitrogen treatment by rushing up to the table, picking me up, and cradling me in her arms. In front of these eminent doctors, she ran out of the room, down the hall, and into the parking lot. I was still in my underpants, covered with giant blisters. She put me in the car and drove me home.

My mother seemed devastated for putting me in that situation and thinking I was in good hands, but I had been tortured. Even worse, I still had all these things living and crawling under my skin.

I can't even begin to tell you what this did to me psychologically. To this day, when I think about it, I can see the image of my skin bubbling. It feels as if there are organisms trying to make their way under my skin, and I'm taken back to those icky, creepy crawling monsters that need to be burned away. This is the feeling that recurs each and every time my OCD is triggered by the thought of germs on my body. Hence, I immediately rush to the sink or shower and spend as long as I can under scalding water, trying to wash away this mental torture.

Clearly the doctors didn't have the answer, so my mom came up with a remedy. Every night after my bath, she would take a dry, rough washcloth with antiseptic solution on it and rub one of the ridges. At first it felt good, because they were itchy. The itchiness would subside. But she would keep rubbing and pressing and rubbing and pressing until eventually the pressure broke the skin and a yellow fluid would ooze out, which was actually the larvae. She would then clean the spot with the antiseptic.

We picked one bump a night, which she rubbed and pressed until it broke open and emptied out. When she had cleaned them all out, the treatment was finished, and the larvae never came back. If I remember correctly, this might have taken a month, but it seemed like an eternity.

In my mind, the nitrogen-on-the-sand-flies was my first performance. My opening act was a person playing with a canister of liquid nitrogen. I was in front of a group of strangers, and it didn't go very well. Though I looked around the room and realized that my show had sold out, it didn't feel good. I just lay there and thought, Oh, my God, this is the horror I've been sentenced to—as I sometimes feel today in the middle of a performance that isn't going well. But I've never stopped a show to admit, "This is not going well . . . good night." Nor has my mom run onto the stage, picked me up, cradled me, and taken me to a safer place. And God knows that's not a bad idea for a closing.

Now remember, the experts believe the first years of your life form who you are. So there I was: a lactose-intolerant, color-blind, urinating outcast who fell into ditches and puddles, sometimes walked like Quasimodo, had a fear of laundry hampers, was a nesting ground for sand flies, and needed 100 percent attention. Welcome to me.

TWO

OCD AND ME

My mind works in strange ways. I have uncontrollable, repetitive thoughts that just won't go away, regardless of how illogical or unreasonable they might be. This is a hallmark for my obsessive-compulsive disorder. I say "my" obsessive-compulsive disorder, as though I own it. I promise you I share it with millions. I don't think I'm alone in saying that we'd rather give it away than share. Once that trigger is pulled, it sets off a reaction that can consume my entire day. That's why I don't shake hands. I used to shake, but it became a trigger. It's one of the many dichotomies of my life: I'm in the public eye, yet I have a fear of shaking hands.

My therapist will sometimes sit with me, hold my hand,

and tell me that I'm supposed to face it, deal with it, and be aware that I'm going to survive. But it's really hard for me to wrap my head around that.

When I do shake hands, my thoughts are the same as many people's. You might think that the person's hand you are touching is covered with germs and you now have those germs on your hand. That's not an abnormal thought. You would wash your hands and go on with your day.

I would have the same thought and go to the sink and wash my hands. But I would make the water hotter than necessary, maybe even scalding, and rub my hands frantically. Then I would dry them and *try* to go on with my day.

But I cannot because I'm obsessed with the fact that those germs are still there, and I have a compulsion to wash my hands continuously. The feeling would be as if the sand fly larvae were crawling under the skin of my hands. I wouldn't be able to focus on anything or even have a conversation until I washed my hands again and again and again and again. It would take several hours to rid myself of those thoughts. Four years ago, I stopped shaking hands. If you come up to me on my book tour and try to shake my hand, I'll know that you haven't read this chapter.

I've always been known as a germaphobe, but the real issue is OCD. According to the National Institute of Mental Health, "Obsessive-Compulsive Disorder, OCD, is an anxiety disorder and is characterized by recurrent, unwanted thoughts (obsessions) and/or repetitive behaviors (compulsions). Repetitive behaviors such as handwashing, counting, checking, or cleaning are often performed with the hope of preventing obsessive thoughts or making them go away." This is uncanny. If there were a place in the dictionary to look up Howie Mandel, it would read, "Howie Mandel is an anxiety disorder and is characterized by recurrent, unwanted thoughts (obsessions) and/or repetitive behaviors (compulsions). Repetitive behaviors such as handwashing, counting, checking, or cleaning are often performed with the hope of preventing obsessive thoughts or making them go away."

I have a seemingly normal life with my wife and three children—at least I'm told they're mine. In my house, the two most commonly uttered sayings are "I love you" and "Wash your hands." People constantly ask me how I maintain a marriage and help raise babies. I can hug, kiss, and touch. My big issues are hands and airborne germs. The use of masks and rubber gloves at opportune times has allowed me to carry on normal relations. I use the word *normal* because I don't know what the real word is. I imagine that until the age of six, my children probably thought their daddy was a surgeon and he just wore work clothes around the house during cold and flu season, which is probably a doctor's busiest time. My mental issues have gone through ebbs and flows. As crazy as this may sound, I have changed diapers. That being said, once all the crap was cleaned and the diaper was on, I refused to shake their hands. As far as my wife goes, I have no issues of touching or kissing. There was a lot of that involved in the making of my three children. However, no matter how amorous I feel, should she sniff or cough I quickly retreat to another part of the house.

Having spent most of my life trying to hide these issues

from the outside world, I long ago learned to embrace the shower as my place of comfort and solace. The state of California has suffered in the past and continues to this day to suffer from a water shortage. I feel somewhat responsible for this. There, I said it.

Back when I was doing *The Howie Mandel Show*, I was still shaking hands. I debated switching to the fist bump but decided to continue shaking because at the time I hadn't revealed publicly that I had any issues. I can't tell you how much just the thought of shaking hands on camera was freaking me out. In any other situation, I could excuse myself and repeatedly scald my hands or go home and suck up the rest of California's water allotment in the shower. But in the midst of a television show, where as the host I had to be there for the entire hour, neither of these options was available. I asked Richard Rosenberg, a friend of mine who's an orthopedic surgeon, to give me surgical soap. Before and after each taping, I would scrub my hands with this medical solution. During that time, I also became aware of Purell and would use vats of it.

Near the end of the run of the talk show, I noticed I had bumps on my hands. I was so freaked. Had I become a nest for the sand fly one more time? I went to a dermatologist, and he explained that these were just warts. A wart is a virus. I had disinfected my hands so much that not only had I killed every germ, I had also killed the antibodies that would fight viruses.

I no longer use the surgical scrub or soak my hands in Purell for hours. I will occasionally use a squirt, and I wash my hands normally. My personal concession is not shaking hands at all, which I admit is a little crazy. I won't touch door-knobs or toilet handles. If by chance you happen to see me in a public restroom, it's like watching a scene out of Cirque du Soleil. I have trained myself to manipulate lids, faucets, and doors with contortions involving maybe just a knee or an elbow. I know what you're thinking. You could end up with *E. coli* on your knee or elbow. But at least it wouldn't be on my hands. This is the logic of OCD. I could sell tickets to my public bathroom contortion performances, but this is one room where I cherish my alone time.

One of the biggest problems I have is meet and greets at my concerts. The purpose of a meet and greet is that in any local market, a radio or TV station runs a contest where you can win tickets to my show, come backstage, meet me, and greet me with a handshake. Before I made any of my mysophobia public, I would put a Band-Aid on my right hand so people wouldn't try to shake it. By the way, mysophobia is a fancy way an author might say "germ pansy." When somebody extended their hand, I would point at the Band-Aid and say, "Look, I can't."

Then they would ask what happened, which I hadn't anticipated. I had just worked really hard onstage coming up with over an hour of comedy, I didn't have much left. My response ranged from "I don't know for sure" to "It's a burn." And then if I said it was a burn, they would ask how I burned myself. It became so mentally cumbersome to come up with a cover story that I was forced to find new tactics.

I went out and bought myself a sling. In my mind, the Band-Aid was pinpointing a specific wound, but a sling is much more general. I thought I could get by with "My shoulder is bothering me." I just thought of something. Why wouldn't I have worn the sling onstage? I truly believed that just having it on after the performance was a great idea.

Stupid idea. I would arrive at the meet and greet with a sling on my right arm. As people still extended their hands to shake mine, I would gesture, "Please, I can't." And without hesitation they would just grab my left hand. Why? Why, people, is it necessary to touch? Let's talk. Let's spend some time together. Here's the deal: Don't touch me. I would spend the rest of the night scalding and scrubbing.

I was boxed in. I couldn't wear two slings, so what could I do? Ah-ha, the fist bump. I didn't come up with the fist bump. The most amazing thing to me was how my little fist became such an alien thing to most people.

I would put out my fist, and they would just stare at it. They would do everything from grabbing and holding on to it to cupping it in their hands. Talk about an awkward moment. I've had people hold their hand out under it as if I were going to release some magic dust. Some people think it's some sort of hip urban handshake. They would hit me on top of the fist, on the bottom, slap the side, and then bang their chest. I have to explain, "It's not BET, it's OCD." But between me, professional sports, and Barack Obama, people now know what it is.

It's debilitating to know I'm not in control of my own mind. It goes places, and I cannot bring it back. People close to me will tell you that during these times I seem agitated or intolerant. The best description is that I feel incredibly busy in my own mind, and that's why I need distraction. That busyness is sometimes torturous.

I know I spend a lot of time making fun of being a germaphobe, which is such a small part of what I deal with each and every day. I've been able to use humor and public awareness to give myself a little comfort. But for the most part, I'm not comfortable at all. It is serious. There are a lot of people who have these issues. OCD can take your life away. People can become suicidal just to escape, though that is not me.

I watched *The Aviator*, Martin Scorsese's biopic on Howard Hughes. At one point in the movie, Hughes is living in isolation, holed up in a dark room, naked, urinating into bottles. To be honest with you, it really scared me, because as weird as this may sound, I promise you it's not a big leap for me to get there. I spend every waking moment trying to control myself, but it's a battle.

Fear is probably the most powerful driving force in my life. I'm always afraid of losing control. I'm afraid of how I feel. I'm afraid of hurting someone else. I'm afraid I'm going to die in the next minute and a half. This is my life.

I feel like a pilot dealing with fear. A trained pilot is supposed to be able to function in the scariest of situations. Consider that US Airways flight that took off from La Guardia and flew into a flock of geese, disabling both engines. Captain Sully Sullenberger, though in the midst of a dire situation, kept his cool and put the plane down safely on the Hudson River. Brace yourself for this analogy. I feel as if the minute I was born, some geese flew into my engines, and I'm just trying to put this life down softly.

The worst thing in the world is to feel isolated, as if I'm the only person who has these feelings. However, a new world has been opened up since the day I talked on *Howard Stern*.

There have been times that I feel totally incapacitated. I keep coming back to Howard Hughes. That's very scary to me. He was phenomenally successful, achieved things in business that were unbelievable, and had great relationships, but then he lost all control. That's my biggest fear in life.

One of the things I can control is not shaking hands. What will be the next thing that I won't be able to do? Or the next thing I can't stop doing, like when I'm compelled to go back and make sure a door is locked ten times?

That really happened. One particular day, I had to be someplace at one o'clock. I left the house, locked the door, and climbed into my car. Then I said to myself, "I don't think I locked the door." So I went back and checked the doorknob. I couldn't open the door, so I knew it was locked. Then I returned to my car, and I thought, Maybe I didn't shake it enough. So I went back, shook it harder, and decided that it was locked.

Back into the car. Even though intellectually I knew I had checked the door, I was obsessed with the fact that it hadn't been locked, and the compulsion to keep checking overtook my logic. I'm not exaggerating when I tell you I got in and out of my car to shake the door maybe ten times. I was mentally paralyzed. I could not move past this.

Eventually, I went to the door and punched it as hard as I could to inflict enough pain on my hand so that when I got back in the car, the throbbing knuckles would send a message to my mind that the door had been checked enough. Needless to say, I was late for that meeting.

That was one of the many moments when my OCD has

taken control of me rather than me controlling it. Here's my fear: That day it was the doorknob. Next it could end up with me naked in a hotel room, urinating into a bottle. If that happens, hopefully it will be a nice, very clean suite with self-locking doors.

I'm not the only one who has to cope with this. It dramatically affects everyone in my life—my wife, my family, my friends. People who have watched me on TV or at live shows often approach my wife and say, "You're so lucky to live with Howie, he must be so much fun." I'm here to tell you, not so much. I would imagine after this book comes out, people will come up to her on the street and hug her. She will be drowning in public empathy.

Seeking help for mental issues doesn't come naturally for many people because of the stigma. It's easy to tell someone at the office, "I'm going to take an hour off to go to the dentist"; no one will think twice about that. But if you happen to tell your co-workers, "I'm going to see my psychiatrist for an hour," they might think you were a crazy person. We'll take care of our dental health, but not our mental health. At this point in our lives, it may be too late to change that thinking. The connotation of therapist or psychiatrist is ingrained. The answer may lie in just changing titles. Maybe it would be easier telling your co-workers, "I've got to take a couple hours off for a little Howie Mandel."

It's just an idea. Hopefully that helps you. And to help me, I'd like to mention one more time something I can't express enough: Here's the deal: Don't touch me.

THREE

A *SENSE* OF HUMOR

As dark, frustrating, or depressing as any moment could possibly be, humor has been my salvation. I have always been fascinated with the *sense* of humor. All the other senses seem to be more definable. Someone who happens to be well dressed must have a strong *sense* of style or fashion. You may judge somebody based entirely on your *sense* of smell: "Larry stinks, so let's not invite him to the party." But humor is different.

The actual *sense* of humor is the ability to sense humor in places where it might not be obvious. I'm not talking about the ability to laugh at jokes or even tell jokes. This *sense* is the ability to find the joke. Some people can find a seed of humor in the darkest, most humiliating moments. I know personally that these moments have made for some of the best stories and material in my act, and judging from the audience's response, I was right.

I have come to believe that humor, more so than the other senses, actually defines who we are. I want to qualify that by saying the lack of a sense of humor doesn't make you a worse or better person. Some of my closest friends and loved ones have absolutely no sense of humor, and I'm okay with that. I just believe that a sense of humor is an identifying factor of who we really are deep inside.

That being said, let me describe my sense of humor. The more awkward, annoying, or humiliating the situation is, the funnier. Many people will say that's mean-spirited and wrong. All comedy is based on being mean-spirited and wrong. Think about it. When a clown falls down and you laugh at him, you're laughing at his misfortune. Within the context of any joke, the humor is based on someone's ignorance, discomfort, and even humiliation.

Let me give you an example. A person goes into a bookstore and buys a book that he thinks might be funny. By the fourth paragraph in chapter 3, he realizes it's a book that describes "what funny is." This idiot has absolutely no idea what he bought. But you see, the joke is on him because I already have his money.

The house I grew up in was filled with humor. My recollections range from my parents playing comedy albums to watching variety shows, talk shows, funny movies, and cartoons. Television has always been a huge part of who I am. Nothing touched me more and shaped my *sense* of humor more than sitting down with my family to watch Allen Funt's *Candid Camera*. With all the other comedy I heard or saw, I knew that something was funny only because my parents were laughing at it or I heard the audience laughing. But I was obviously too young to understand what was going on. Watching *Candid Camera* was different. Not only did I understand it, but it became my sensibility.

On the show, Allen Funt would tell us the prank he was going to play on someone and then leave us to see how this poor victim would react. I understand that funny is subjective. What's funny to one person may not be funny to another. When I was six, funny to me was the fact that Allen Funt and the audience were just pretending something and the poor victim thought it was real. I wasn't laughing at the jokes; I was laughing at the fact that the victim didn't know he was part of a joke.

This set off a spark in my head. The show ignited my sense of humor. From that day forward, if I could purposefully put somebody in an awkward, uncomfortable, or embarrassing situation, or watch someone in an awkward, uncomfortable, or embarrassing situation, my funny bone was tickled. I know what you are thinking: Howie Mandel has the sense of humor of a six-year-old. And you know what I say? Correct.

After I saw *Candid Camera*, there was no turning back. At school I tried to do the same things, just without a camera or an audience. I would see a stranger on a bench, sit uncomfortably close to him, and make horrible, high-pitched noises just to watch the person's reaction. It was my private candid camera. That person never thought I was funny. At best, he just thought I was annoying. I'd get a dirty look as he'd walk away. Boy, would I laugh—just me alone. I thought I had done the best joke in the world because that person had no idea that I was just kidding. Neither did anyone else. I learned years later that I had left out a critical step . . . an audience. Did I entertain? No. I just annoyed. Come to think of it, comedians often say, "If I can make only one person laugh, I'm doing my job." But I don't think they mean the one person should be the comedian.

I couldn't help myself. I constantly did—and still do—things like this without any sense of consequence. Most kids at that age just want to fit in and be like everybody else. You can imagine that this kind of behavior resulted in my being regarded as a mental case by my peers. Even when I said I was kidding with my pranks, people didn't know what the joke was. I thought being funny would make people accept me. This was my way of feeling accepted by people. I wanted you laughing at me or laughing with me. But these impulsive, futile attempts at humor ended up alienating me even more. Let's just say that I had a lot of time to myself, which is not good for someone suffering from OCD.

Even though I was miserably alone because of these impulsive shenanigans, I didn't seem to have the power to stop them. I remember one time in middle school during recess standing by myself, watching everyone else interact on the playground. Rather than wallowing in my loneliness, I became impulsively fixated on a ladder leading to my second-floor math class, which was about to begin. It had obviously been left there by the custodian washing the windows. The bell ending recess rang. All the children cleared the playground, heading to their respective classes. Without a thought, I headed toward the ladder.

After what I believed was enough time for the class to get settled, I began to climb toward my classroom. As I reached the second-floor window, I could see the kids focused on the teacher writing on the blackboard. I gripped the window from the outside and began to push it up. Apparently, the noise of the window sliding up caused a shift in the class's attention. The teacher stopped writing and looked my way, along with twenty-something other heads. I lifted my body off the ladder and onto the ledge of the window. I casually lowered myself to the floor, wandered over to my seat, and sat down as if nothing had happened.

Again, I had failed to let anyone in on my little escapade. Had I, this might have been considered funny. But instead I was considered insane by the masses.

The proceedings were obviously brought to a halt. Followed by what seemed like an eternity of awkward silence, the teacher boomed, "Howard Mandel!"

I looked up at him with all the innocence I could conjure, as if to say, "Why in heaven's name would you be calling on me?"

"Do you have an explanation?"

I responded very earnestly, "Normally I would, sir, but I happened to miss the first ten minutes of class."

"Stand up!"

I stood up.

"Would you like to share with us?"

I reached into my pocket and pulled out my Popeye Pez dispenser and started making my way down the row to give everyone a Pez candy. Before I could get the second one out, he screamed, "Out in the hall!"

Needless to say, I ended up missing much more than ten minutes of that class, or many classes, for that matter. I remember discovering that I had the capacity to do a baby voice, which would later become the character "Bobby." Again with the teacher writing on the board, I would pipe up in a babyish falsetto, "Help me! Help me, please!" Without even turning his head, he would say, "Howard, out in the hall!" A good portion of my academic career was spent in the hall.

On that particular day, I remember the principal saying to me, "What good can you get out of this kind of behavior, Howard?"

I wish I could find him today and tell him I don't know if it's good, but it's a paragraph in this book.

No one understood my humor. The most common sound I heard as a child in school was "tch," followed by an eye roll. I don't know how to write that sound. The girls would always exhale in disgust and go, "Tch," because what I did was never in the context of a joke. I get the fact that nobody liked it because I was doing things you are not supposed to do. The fact that you are not supposed to do them is what made them funny to me.

In middle school, I felt as if I were a pariah. I had no real friends, so I began attending a teen club on Friday nights at another school, Dufferin Heights Junior High. I became known as the guy who would do outrageous things. I was kind

of a prop. Bring Howard, he will do whatever we want. And I would.

As much as I wanted to be funny, my real goal was to meet girls. But at the time, I looked like and sounded like a girl. I had curly hair down to my shoulders and a high-pitched voice, and I still hadn't shaved. I stood four feet ten and weighed eighty-five pounds. Oh, my God, I just realized that I was Hannah Montana.

This proved to be an asset. I could walk into the girls' bathroom, stand at the mirror, and brush my hair without anyone thinking there was a boy in the room. And it was a great way to meet girls. It was probably the first time I set eyes on my future wife.

I was never that great with the ladies. My first memory of setting my sights on someone was in Mr. Cave's class in the sixth grade. Her name was Vivian Sher, and she was my first crush. Today, I believe that she has no idea I existed or was even in her class.

I had no concept of what to do, I just knew that she was a

beautiful girl and I wanted her—though I didn't know what that meant. I didn't know how to talk to her. I don't think I ever said three words to her.

One day, I devised a way into her heart. I didn't really devise it, because again, the way I operate is that I don't think ahead. ADHD is a beautiful thing. It was after school, and I was in a trance. Vivian left school, and I followed her. She lived at the corner of Bathurst and Sheppard, which was not in the same direction as, or anywhere near, my house. Basically, I stalked her. She walked home, and I followed about a hundred yards behind her. Without ever turning or even acknowledging that I was there, Vivian entered her building, and I just stood outside and stared. I didn't have a plan. I didn't know what I was doing, and I had no idea how this would gain me her companionship. I stood for what must have been an eternity.

I eventually went home and got yelled at for coming home late. I had walked two miles out of my way. That was the extent of my relationship with Vivian Sher. I never followed her again, and I never said a word to her. The next time I mentioned Vivian Sher's name was right now in this book. I just want to say I probably wanted to continue my pursuit, but as you can see, I probably lost focus and went off in many other directions on the road to building the monument that would become me.

At this point in my life, my only friend was my humor, and I desperately needed someone to share it with. As I entered high school, I continued on my quest to meet a woman. I believed that the path to a woman was sports. The jock always got the girl.

I know what you're thinking: How could I be a jock? I'm only four feet ten and eighty-five pounds. But remember, now I'm in high school. I'm a totally different person. I've grown up. I'm now four feet ten and a half inches and eighty-six pounds . . . with long, flowing locks. The word *jock* doesn't fit that image unless you add an *e* and a *y* on the end of the word *jock*. Unfortunately, this wasn't part of the curriculum. That being said, I can't tell you how many times I showed up at school wearing brightly colored, shiny clothes.

I had to join one of the existing school teams. A team that needed someone with not only my athletic prowess and my dwarflike dimensions, but my ability to work alone. Lo and behold, the Greco-Roman wrestling team. I really didn't care about the sport, but I truly believed that any female who laid her eyes on me in the Northview Heights official athletic uniform would be mine for the taking. Again, I never think ahead as far as the consequences of my actions are concerned.

I made the team. The prerequisite for making the team was to fill the void in the under-ninety-pound weight class. I was given my uniform. Who the hell would imagine that the uniform for Greco-Roman-style wrestling was a f—ing onesie?

In my dreams, I believed this was my ticket to end up in the arms of a beautiful woman. Instead, I ended up in the arms of another ninety-pound guy trying to roll me around on the filthy floor while I was wearing what looked like a one-piece bathing suit belonging to a beautiful woman.

The only task the coach gave me was to remain under ninety pounds. There were times when I tipped the scale at ninety-two pounds and had only hours to get back to my fighting weight. This was achieved by wrapping my entire body in plastic garbage bags and running until I lost over two pounds of liquid weight—or, as the layman refers to it, dehydration. My mother eventually made me quit the team. I don't want anybody to believe my parents were not supportive. They attended many of my matches, watched me get pinned within thirty-five seconds, and then frequently drove me to the hospital to be x-rayed.

My quest for female companionship never let up. A family friend, who owned one of the biggest bingo halls in Canada, gave me a job selling sandwiches and drinks. On most bingo nights there were probably two thousand people, mostly old ladies, playing bingo for thousands of dollars.

My mom happily drove me to work. I actually remember the drive to work because guys would pull up next to us at the red light, honk their horns, and make signals. I would wave back, thinking, Who are these guys? It took a while, but my mother and I eventually realized that they thought I was a girl and they were trying to pick me up. Truthfully, I didn't think that I looked like that much of a girl without my wrestling uniform.

Once I was inside the bingo hall, there was no mistaking the man in me. I had a metal cart on wheels that was loaded down with cases of soda and egg salad sandwiches. I wore a white shirt with a bow tie and a paper hat, which I cocked to the side. This was not the uniform of a lady. I swear to you to this day, I was so excited about my look. I thought, Wait until the ladies get a load of me! I had a tie, a paper hat, and egg salad sandwiches.

I was going to make money and look good doing it, so much so that I actually invited girls to come and watch me. I had no sense of what looked good or even how to get a girl. I walked around with the stupidest expression on my face, but I wasn't trying to be funny. I remember looking in the mirror at my hair flared out from the sides of my cocked hat, thinking, This guy's hot. I had the looks, the swagger, and all the egg salad you could want. What more did a woman need in a man?

Once I brought a girl to watch me sell egg salad in the bingo hall. Actually, I told a friend to come and watch me, and he brought the girl. But I thought she was there to see me—even though she was his girlfriend. So I set out to impress.

The first bingo games were for $50, followed by a special game played before the break for $1,000. At that time, they didn't use punch-out cards the way they do today. The players had see-through plastic chips that looked like tiddlywinks. I knew that the game was almost ending. The moment somebody yelled, "Bingo!" I was supposed to be in the middle of the hall, where everyone could buy refreshments. If I was late getting to the designated spot, the owner would lose sales. So I loaded up my cart with sodas and egg salad, checked my tie, and cocked my hat. My boss told me that I had better hurry, so I figured I would run.

First, I charted a path that would take me past this girl. It was nearing the end of a $1,000 game, and tension in the room was building as two thousand people were listening for the next number that might thrust any one of them into the financial stratosphere. I took off like lightning, gaining speed, heading in her direction. In my mind, when she heard the *whoosh* of my cart streaking by, she would look up dreamily at egg salad boy with the paper hat.

What was I thinking? As I retell this story, I can't tell you how serious I was. I wasn't trying to be funny. I was dead serious. It's not as though I didn't see myself. I had actually checked in the mirror seconds earlier to make sure I looked my best and had seen the image of a five-foot, ninety-pound man-girl garden gnome with a paper hat and thought . . . perfect.

With my hair blowing in the wind and a glint in my eye, I ran right by her. I watched the excitement as her eyes locked . . . on N-44. She never even looked up. But then I made my right turn down the aisle toward the center of the hall. When I say "I made the right turn," I mean *I* made the right turn. The cart did not. With the speed that I was traveling and the weight of the cart, physics took over. The cart hit the corner of a long table where five hundred people were sitting. Instead of hearing the next number, they heard a smashing, explosive sound, followed by old ladies screaming and chips flying all over the floor. It was one of the most embarrassing nights of my life.

At that point the girl may have looked up at me, but I assure you she didn't go home with me. No one ever did. At least I was consistent. I can't even imagine taking a woman home at this point in my life. We were now living in an apartment. I was sharing a room with my brother and living with my parents. The sound of a giggly girl and the smell of egg salad would be disconcerting to any roommate, to say the least. I left that job shortly after it began.

Speaking of consistency, I consistently lost jobs no matter how much I enjoyed them. In the summer of 1970, I found a job working at the Canadian National Exhibition, the annual summer fair in Toronto. It was also my first foray into show business. I operated a ride called the Vegas Chase. It was a ride that went around and around and around. I don't know why I wrote that, because what ride doesn't? There are no rides that just go straight and never come back. On the Vegas Chase, you sat in an egg-shaped pod with pictures of dice on it and went in circles quickly.

I loved my job. I wore an orange jumpsuit with a little clown emblem and the word *Conklin* on the right pocket. Conklin was the guy who operated all the rides at the exhibition, so I was working for Conklin. I would sit on a tractor seat with a microphone in one hand and the lever controlling the ride in the other. This was so much better than the paper hat and the egg salad. Again, I thought every girl was looking at me.

I took such joy when people screamed. I would say, "Do you want to go faster?" and they would all yell, "Yes!" I was performing, and I was in control. But this didn't seem to be enough for me. I had to take it one step too far. I decided to make it my personal *Candid Camera*, without thinking of the ramifications.

In the midst of the ride loaded with people and whirling at about thirty miles per hour, I would scream into the microphone, "Do you want to go faster?!" They would scream back at me, "Yes!" Pushing the lever even farther, I'd scream, "Even faster?!" "Yes!" Then out of left field, I would scream, "Secure your orange shoulder harnesses, we are going upside down in five seconds!" I would begin the countdown: "Five . . . four . . ."

Here's the deal: There were no orange shoulder harnesses, and the ride didn't go upside down, but they didn't know that.

The screams began to sound different. It might have been the sound of terror.

"Three . . . two . . ."

The screams were accompanied by heads jerking to the left and right and hands reaching desperately over shoulders, grabbing aimlessly at something that didn't exist. I also could hear people scream, "Help me! Please, I can't find my harness."

Nobody was having fun . . . except for me.

This lasted a couple of days. Not my enjoyment—the job.

My spectacles became legendary in small circles. During this time period, kids in my area hung out at Howard Johnson's. I would go and sit alone in a booth. Every booth was packed with groups of eight or ten people, yet I'd sit alone. I would put on a ridiculous accent and set my volume control on loud. Everybody watched as the waitress approached. The waitress was usually a woman in her sixties with no patience or sense of humor. Remember, she was serving sixteen-year-olds at two a.m.

I would proceed to order my favorite dessert, which at the time was a Fudgana, a banana split covered with fudge. So it's "fudge" and "banana," but with my accent, I could make "fudgana" sound eerily close to "vagina." My goal was to see how many times this loudmouthed foreign exchange student could scream, "Vagina!" into the face of this sixty-year-old woman before being asked to leave.

It would go something like this.

She would ask, "May I help you?"

I would say, "Doo yoo ave vagina?"

She would ask, "What?"

I would explain, "I would like yooo vagina."

She would say, "What are you saying?"

"I saw picture your vagina in menu. I vant eat your vagina." As I was screaming, "I vant your vagina," the entire restaurant would be rolling in laughter. I would maintain an innocent, fish-out-of-water demeanor. "Why can't I ave yooo vagina?"

I want to make two points. First, the record was thirty-one. Second, I was always asked to leave and ended up home alone. You may be reading this and thinking this is very juvenile, but I was only sixteen years old. That being said, I would do exactly the same thing today.

Through these spectacles, I started to garner some friends and began to spread my social wings. I got invited to a party at Lizzie Zuckerbrot's house. As usual, I just sat on the floor, not knowing what I should do at a party. I wasn't really mingling because I'm not a mingler. To my left was a guy wearing Coke-bottle aviator glasses who also seemed to be a nonmingler. His name was Michael Rotenberg.

The walls of the room were covered with pictures of Lizzie and the entire Zuckerbrot family. The pictures were various shapes and sizes. By looking at them, you could tell that it took years and years to create these memories, not to mention the display itself.

The party seemed to drift into another room, leaving Michael and me alone. We didn't say anything to each other as we got up and walked toward the pictures. We started removing the pictures from the wall and placing them on the floor.

Once all the pictures had been removed, I noticed the look of blank walls covered with an irregular pattern of what seemed like hundreds of nails. And now, ladies and gentlemen, the pièce de résistance: I removed one of the nails.

As if nothing had happened, Michael and I sat down and waited until Lizzie Zuckerbrot and the rest of the partygoers migrated back into the room. There was a shriek of horror as Lizzie Zuckerbrot realized that the Zuckerbrot family collage had been destroyed.

The party took a dark turn. Michael and I remained calmly on the floor as every other party guest began to join the frenzy of trying to put back all the pictures before her parents returned home.

Lizzie Zuckerbrot assembled the pictures on the wall according to her memory. After almost an hour, Lizzie was down to the final two pictures. The end was in sight. The second-to-last picture made its way onto the wall. One picture remained. One picture and no nail.

Lizzie Zuckerbrot became even more determined. She had an idea. "Let's remove all the pictures and start from scratch," she said.

Another hour passed and Lizzie Zuckerbrot was once again down to the last picture. Now, I don't know if this is true, but I think Lizzie Zuckerbrot is solely responsible for that famous saying "If at first you don't succeed, try, try again." Because that's exactly what she did. Michael and I could not contain ourselves as we watched her remove the pictures for the third time.

This went on for the entire evening. For the life of me, I can't remember how it ended. But Michael was one of the first people who seemed to share my sensibility: finding humor in others' duress. He quickly became one of my best friends.

Years later, after he finished law school in Canada, Michael moved to Los Angeles and became my lawyer. Today, he is still my best friend, my manager, and a co-owner of 3 Arts Entertainment, a major Hollywood management and production company.

At this point, I became something of a social butterfly. I was attending parties, hanging out with various groups, and solidifying friendships that remain to this day: Michael Rotenberg, Jeff Weiman, and my nearest and dearest, Terry Soil, who is now known as Terry Mandel. It took her years just to say yes to going on a date with me, not for my lack of trying.

Terry was always around. She was blond and beautiful and five feet six without heels. I was just breaking five feet without heels. In my mind, we were the perfect match. I would try to talk to her, but she wouldn't have anything to do with me. I don't think it was only because I was half a foot shorter than her—I also had a reputation of being an out-of-control, crazy person. I wish I'd had the foresight to tell her that one day I would be asked to write a book and I would mention her.

Lo and behold, I finally had a breakthrough and we set a date for a Friday night. She had very strict stipulations for the date. Number one, it had to be a double date. Number two, she would be with Jeff Mintz and I would be with another girl. But I could still say, "I went out last Friday with Terry Soil."

Days passed. Weeks passed. Months passed. Maybe even a year passed. And then one particular day in 1973, she was okay with going out with just me alone. I would imagine for her it was out of a lack of anything else to do, but I can't tell you how excited I was. It was a very special night.

I needed to prepare. I took out my favorite pair of jeans and my squirt gun. I filled the squirt gun with Clorox bleach. I put the jeans on a table and began squirting the outline of a tongue protruding from my fly on the pants. In minutes, the blue had disappeared and I had a white tongue hanging off of my crotch.

As I look at that paragraph, I'm with you, people—it's not funny, it's not tasteful, it's ridiculous. But then remember, I never think, I just do.

Like a gentleman, I drove to her house to pick her up. I arrived on time. I rang the doorbell. Terry came to the door, looked at my groin, and didn't say a word. Luckily, she was standing between me and her mother, who came around the corner to ask Terry who this young lady was. It was me, Howard Mandel.

I don't think her mother ever noticed my groin, and Terry never mentioned the tongue on my jeans. She quietly got into my mom's Cutlass Supreme convertible, a real cool car on a real cold night. I was feeling great.

We were heading to a movie, and the roads were terrible. I remember I made a left turn onto Bathurst Street as the rear tires must have hit a patch of ice. The car began to fishtail. The back end swung around the front and kept going, sending the car into a tailspin. This whole experience felt like slow motion. My eyes were bulging. I saw headlights—spinning—taillights. I saw a tree, then a curb, then a bus, then headlights again. I was in my own little *Fast and the Furious: Tokyo Drift*.

And then the two wheels on the passenger side slammed up against the curb. The car was catapulted up on its side, about to roll over. I thought we were going to die. Time seemed to stand still as the car teetered on two wheels, slammed back down, bounced once, and came to rest on all four wheels.

My heart was pounding so fast, I thought it would come out of my chest. I looked over at Terry to make sure she was all right. She seemed to be all in one piece except for the fact that her arms were crossed and her face was contorted.

After a long pause, the first two words off her lips were "Very funny."

Wait, did I just hear her right? Did she think this was a joke? No matter how profusely I denied it, she was convinced that I had almost flipped the car and killed us for a joke—which pretty much sums up my reputation.

It's also why I don't have a GED. To this day, I'm upset I didn't finish high school or go to college. I constantly acted out impulsively.

In high school at Northview Heights, I did everything from throwing a chocolate bar in the pool to make it look as if someone defecated (and then I dove in and ate it) to hiring contractors to give unauthorized bids on an extension to the library. I disrupted so many other activities and classes that school officials called in a psychologist for testing. As an adult, I have been diagnosed with ADHD, which in my case manifests itself in trouble focusing, impulsive behavior, and basically everything that eventually curtailed my academic career. But the psychologist just chalked it up to having a bad attitude—obviously ADHD didn't seem to be recognized in the early 1970s.

As luck would have it, I ended up contracting mononucleosis and missing class for three months. I fell so far behind, I had to leave Northview. I enrolled myself in another school that was on the semester system in order to catch up, but within weeks they found out I didn't live in the district and had me removed.

I ended up at Georges P. Vanier Secondary School, where things quickly went downhill. I had a friend who knew someone in a university medical program where they dissected cadavers. The friend of a friend gave me a human foot, which of course I packed in my gym bag, brought to school, and left in someone's shoe in the locker room during PE. The energy it took for me to come up with and execute these extravagant stunts far outweighed the energy and time I was putting into academics, which eventually fell by the wayside.

My educational career was over. Where was I to turn? I was the only one I knew at my age who didn't have a place to get dressed and go each and every morning. Who was the joke on now?

This was a lonely, scary moment in my life. One of the things that got me through it was that my parents continued to love, encourage, and support me in every way. They connected with a friend in the carpet business. I got a job at Carpet Liquidators, apparently my only option for the future. I was selling carpet. I was a bona fide full-time carpet salesman. Let's get this straight: I was a bona fide full-time, color-blind carpet salesman. Wait, there's more: I was a bona fide full-time, color-blind carpet salesman with an insatiable need to be the center of attention. And here is how it manifested itself.

The customers were called *ups*. There were three or four salesmen, and we would take turns attending to the customer. Whenever it was my up, I would put on a performance for the other salesmen. First and foremost, I wanted to entertain myself and the people at the office.

This was not much different from any given night at Howard Johnson's. I would have the other salesmen stand close enough so they could overhear me. I would do everything from talking gibberish to positioning myself awkwardly just to see if I could elicit a reaction. Making the sale was secondary to getting the laugh.

I had business cards made up where my name on the card was "Howard Men." Whenever customers decided to make a purchase, I would ask them to step into my office. I could see the look on their faces as we approached the door that said "Men." I would invite them into my office very professionally, open up a private stall, lower the seat, and ask them to make themselves comfortable while we completed the contract. Most people were so off-kilter that they wouldn't even ask why they were sitting on a toilet filling out an order.

I was constantly consumed with my own pranks. I had no sense of boundaries. There was no teacher to tell me to stop. At the time, I had started dating Terry regularly. She was one of the first people who understood my sense of humor and enjoyed being in on the joke. I like to say we began dating. She describes it as going to a show every night. Eventually, she was forced to set boundaries.

The first boundary came when I was with her at a department store makeup counter. She was chatting with a saleslady. I didn't happen to be the center of attention, so I was getting bored. Like a six-year-old, when I get bored, stuff happens.

I started putting my fingers in the makeup testers. Each finger became caked with a different color. Terry concluded her purchase, then we left the counter and began strolling through the mall. I became very amorous, pinched her face, and started whispering sweet nothings, like "Look at you . . . aren't you cute today." Then I touched her nose with another finger and whispered, "Look at that little button nose, you're such a doll." Each statement and each touch left a different mark.

As we continued through the mall, the mess on her face grew. Within minutes, she looked like a crazy Indian, causing people to stare at her as they whisked by. Terry seemed to notice the stares, but I believe she interpreted them as if the people were mesmerized by a supermodel passing in their midst. Her walk developed into a swagger, as if to say, "I look so hot today that people can't keep their eyes off me." It actually reminded me of the attitude I had wearing the paper hat pushing the egg salad cart. At that point, I probably should've told her what I had done. But that's the problem with me: I never quite know when to quit.

I told her that I just remembered I wanted to buy something for my mother and we would need to head back to the makeup counter. I started running back through the mall like an idiot. There was no reason to be running, but because I was running, she chased me, yelling, "Why are you running? Where are you going?"

Now you have to picture this: There is a guy running through the mall like a crazy person, being chased by a young lady wearing messed-up war paint.

We were both out of breath by the time we arrived at the makeup counter. The saleslady asked if she could help us, all the while looking incredulously over my shoulder at the spectacle that was Terry.

"Yes," I said. "I don't know how to say this, but my girlfriend has trouble applying makeup."

The saleslady looked at Terry's multicolored, streaked face and didn't say anything.

Terry spoke up. "No, I don't," she said adamantly—as if she were defending her makeup job. Now Terry looked at me, burning a hole in the back of my head and thinking, What the f— are you talking about?

"Well, you do," I said.

"I do not," she shot back. "I know exactly what I'm doing. Why are you saying that?"

Terry was so annoyed with me that she turned to walk away. In that moment, she caught a glimpse of her profile in a mirror and realized what had happened. She swung her purse as hard as she could, slamming me on the shoulder, and then stormed out of the department store.

She was really upset. So was I. I thought I had lost my girlfriend through my antics, giving no consideration to the consequences. Terry made me promise never to play a practical joke on her again. She was to be considered out of bounds, so that meant that I could not do things to her, but I could do things with her.

I remained in the carpet business for a few years and eventually opened up my own company, National Broadloom Sales. National Broadloom Sales consisted of one room and a phone. I would take out ads advertising a shop-at-home service. And as calls came in, I would answer the phone with various voices that made the operation seem much bigger than it actually was.

The receptionist was me in a falsetto voice saying, "National Broadloom." When someone asked to speak to a salesperson, I would accidentally transfer her to the warehouse, which was me in a low voice saying, "Warehouse." But if the customer said she was looking for a salesman, I would reconnect her to my regular voice, answering, "Sales," and make an appointment to go to the house and show her my wares.

Terry was my first truly captive audience. After either school or work, she used to come with me on these sales calls. My goal was to see how outrageous I could be at the same time I made a living. Once in the home, I would have the family or the customer select the color and style of carpet they wanted. Next I would explain that I had to take measurements.

One particular time, I proceeded to take off my shirt. I was standing there bare-chested. You can't imagine the awkwardness the family felt at the sight of a strange, bare-chested man standing in their living room, getting ready to measure for the carpet. The discomfort was palpable. I can't tell you how many times they just looked back and forth at one another in silence. I know they wanted to flee, but this was their house. I took a pen and drew the room on my stomach, noting the measurements. As soon as I finished, I had the family sit on the couch, while I lay at their feet with the floor plan and my nipples facing up at them.

Pointing to the rooms I had drawn on my chest, I said, demonstrating, "See this room that starts at my belly button? That is the family room. You want earth-tone shag to go up here just below my left nipple." But I knew that's not where they wanted the earth-tone shag, it was where they wanted the brown Berber, so they stopped me.

"No, sir, that's not right."

"Okay, show me where you want the shag."

At first, it was really uncomfortable for this poor lovely family, but eventually it was like "This must be how you buy carpet." The conversation slowly evolved into a sense of normalcy. The husband remarked, "You see where your left nipple is? That's where we want the Berber to start." Then the wife cut in, "Honey, no, I think the earth-tone shag should go from his belly button to his right nipple." All the while, their young daughter would be saying, "Mommy, why does the carpet man not have a . . ." At that moment, her mother would shush her, as if she were being rude.

I learned from this that people would rather suffer in awkward hell than be embarrassed by standing their ground and saying, "What the fuck is going on?" It was too dangerous because I was in their home and they couldn't escape, so they just made this world real and comfortable. Thank you, Allen Funt.

Another time, I was called up to measure a massive house. I pulled out a six-inch ruler and began measuring. My goal was to see how long they would let me stay. I put the ruler on the floor, held my finger at the end, and then mumbled to myself, "Two," flipped it over, and said, "Three."

The man of the house interrupted and told me he had a tape measure, to which I held up my hand and said, "Please, please. I've lost count. I have to use my own equipment." And I would start again, "One . . . two . . . three."

The atmosphere was always so uncomfortable. Nobody would ever confront me during these stunts. They would just sit there and endure it in total discomfort, which is my favorite kind of comedy. I consider those sales to be the first time I was being paid for comedy. These were my shows. Nobody was booking me in a club, but I was invited to perform at someone's house and I was getting paid for it.

FOUR

YUK YUK'S

Up to this point, you might think I was putting myself on the path toward becoming a comedian. I promise you there couldn't have been anything further from my mind. All these shenanigans were just impulsive bursts of misbehavior that happened to garner some laughs. As it turns out, they were simply a product of who I was—a twenty-two-year-old ADHD-OCD-laden color-blind carpet salesman desperately in need of attention at any expense.

I was still living with my parents in a two-bedroom apartment in suburban Toronto. Show business was not part of my psyche. I knew absolutely nothing about show business. At the time, my idea of show business would've been selling television sets.

My only previous foray into the arts had been in high school. After failing numerous academic courses, I picked up a class in theater arts for what I believed would be an easy pass. Our teacher, Mr. Brown, would have us dress in black and curl up into a ball as if we were a seed. He would drop the needle on a Simon and Garfunkel record and instruct us to bloom slowly to the music. As Paul and Art's music filled the room, I lifted my head and began to bloom. The girl to my right also began blooming, spreading her petals. This caused my stem to rise. Apparently, my plant was sprouting a new branch. That's about all I remember from theater arts, except for the fact that I got a C in blooming.

Everybody else I knew was charting a path to their future. I wasn't charting, nor did I have a path. But I did have a goal. I wanted to be a millionaire. I wasn't saving money. Anything I made went directly into my pockets. Anything I wanted emptied my pockets.

My impulsiveness didn't serve me well in business. While running National Broadloom Sales, I decided I needed a marketing campaign. I went to the local paper to buy ads. I was told that if I signed a contract to guarantee them fifty-two half-page ads in a year, I would receive a discount. Impulsively, I signed the contract without any thought. That's not true. My one thought was that I was on my way to making a million dollars. Every week for fifty-two weeks, my company would have a huge ad. Every week for fifty-two weeks, as per the contract, I had to pay thousands and thousands of dollars. Every week for fifty-two weeks, I didn't earn thousands and thousands of dollars. Needless to say, I was on my way to losing a million dollars. National Broadloom Sales eventually closed its doors. Make that its door.

My frenzied, scattershot behavior became my modus operandi. Within days, I reopened as North American Carpet Sales—another room, another phone, but now I was going to take the entire continent by storm. Within months, it was a mere cog in the wheel of the conglomerate that became well-known . . . to me as HMI, Howard Mandel International. I sold smoke detectors, tied up the rights to a toothbrush you could floss with, and began selling novelty items, such as the Uncle Sherman Flasher Doll. This was a toy I had seen on one of my family trips to Miami. It was a stuffed old man in a trench coat that when opened revealed his package. This was certainly going to make me my million.

I believe this entrepreneurial spirit was inspired by my dad. He was the greatest, most optimistic father anybody could ever have, always brimming with new ideas and fearless about executing them. This eventually made him the proprietor of a very successful commercial lighting company, which is the business my brother runs to this day.

But throughout his career, there were many fun detours, each of which holds a warm and fuzzy place in my heart. He started as a cabdriver, then sold cars, stocks, and diamonds. I remember the times he would bring home new inventions to market. The two that stand out are the water softeners and Zip Grip. I have no idea what a water softener is. The Zip Grip was a way of hanging your laundry on the line without using clothespins.

At this time, most people relied on a laundry line hanging

in the backyard or basement rather than a clothes dryer. Zip Grip was an aluminum pulley system that used two lines and a row of bearings that would twist as you pulled the line. My father decided he could market this to the world. My entire family would sit on the living room floor and pack flyers into envelopes for mass mailings.

I never saw my father discouraged, regardless of the results. All I remember is the excitement we felt embarking on new adventures. When I was about thirteen or fourteen years old, he bought a hotel in Stratford, Ontario. The entire town is modeled after Great Britain's Stratford-upon-Avon and is home to Canada's foremost Shakespearean festival. The hotel, the Avon, was named after the famous river. I only remember visiting it twice.

This hotel seemed to be a small building with maybe ten rooms. The actual business was the bar downstairs. Both of my visits were to one of the rooms in the hotel. I was never actually in the bar. I can now tell you why.

My father had a great sense of humor, and like Shakespeare, he appreciated theater. Now, remember where we are. At any given time during the festival, you could see *Macbeth* or *Romeo and Juliet*. Not to be outdone, my father would feature an act by the name of Princess Glow.

I was never allowed to see the act, but I did see the picture. Princess Glow was a young lady weighing in at approximately 350 pounds. Her performance consisted of getting naked and taking a bubble bath in a giant champagne glass positioned center stage. For the grand finale, she would climb out of the champagne glass—which in itself was impressive. Remember, she weighed 350 pounds dry, and now she was soapy, wet, and slippery. She would leave the stage and walk throughout the audience, dropping her huge wet soapy breasts on the heads of unsuspecting bald men. Et tu, Brute? This was the show my dad produced.

Here's the deal with this. While doing research for this book, I asked my mom if my dad really ran a strip bar. Her reply was "No, he had bands, too." The truth is it really wasn't a strip bar. Forty-six weeks a year, he hired bands and maybe a comic, but for maybe six weeks, he had acts like Princess Glow. In my mind, once you have a naked woman dropping her breasts on your customers' heads, it's a strip bar.

It's like—and not to be derogatory toward anyone gay—if a man has sex with six other men but also from time to time there are women, then I would say that man has gay tendencies. Just like my mom can't say it wasn't a strip bar because he had strippers for only six weeks. Is that a good analogy? Probably not.

Back to the point at hand. I believe my father is the genesis of my entrepreneurial spirit.

I opened up a storefront selling carpet remnants downtown across the street from the YMCA. I can't even imagine who occupied this space before I moved in. The store was about fifteen feet deep from the sidewalk and three and a half feet wide. Every morning, I opened the front door, threw some remnants on the sidewalk, and stood there waiting for customers. Sometimes after school, Rotenberg would come by and relieve me.

More than the money—and I use that term loosely—the

draw to this venture was the vagrants living at the Y. It sounds very charitable, but I was fascinated and could sit for hours with drug addicts, alcoholics, and the mentally deranged. I would have groups of them gather around me and regale me with their adventures. Unlike my friends, I didn't have to get up early in the morning to go to school, so just about every night after dropping Terry off, I would spend time in dough-nut shops being mesmerized by the people of the night.

One particular character that comes to mind is a middle-aged man who used to sit beside me each and every night and order a jelly doughnut. He would squeeze it as he was bring-ing it up to his face. The pressure of the squeeze would force the jelly to protrude from a hole on the side. He would start talking at the jelly as if it were a friend: "Thanks for coming out, I've been meaning to tell you something." As he reached the end of the sentence, he would release the pressure, caus-ing jelly to recoil back into the doughnut. At this point, he would scream at the top of his lungs, "Don't you fucking walk away from me when I'm talking to you!"

I found these times and moments to be my favorite source of entertainment, mostly because they were real, unscripted slices of life. No movie, television show, or joke could surpass this natural form of entertainment. It was like living in two different worlds. I would work all day in one world, meet friends, and go to dinner. Once they went home, I would cat-apult myself into a parallel universe populated by the de-ranged characters of the night.

And then it was back to Mommy and Daddy's house. Once home, I washed my hands incessantly and took countless scalding showers. The showers were preceded by the gathering of towels. One was laid out on the floor. One was used to wrap my filthy clothes. The third was used to dry myself and shield my hands as I picked up the remaining towels so that I could lift the lid of the laundry hamper to dispose of everything, having touched nothing—not my clothes, not even the hamper or its contents. All this before I would make my way into my bed. Finally, lying there blotched and chafed, fresh from my scalding shower, looking back on my evening, I'd think, Boy, were *those* people crazy.

On nights when I didn't go out, weird and wonderful thoughts would fill my head. Very late in the evening, I would go into my parents' bedroom and stand at the foot of their bed to share. Sometimes I would stand there for a half hour just doing the Bobby the Baby voice. I would constantly elicit laughter until my father would say, "Howie, please, we need to sleep." I can only imagine what was going through their heads. All their friends' children, along with my friends, either were away at college or had started careers. The point is, at this age they were certainly not living at home. My younger brother was in college studying electronic technology. Here were Albert and Evelyn Mandel trying to sleep as their twenty-two-year-old son told funny little stories—until they sent him to his room.

As I write about my life at this age, I'll be honest in telling you that I feel somewhat embarrassed. If I'd taken out a personal ad at that point, it would have read something like this: "Howard Mandel, 22-year-old entrepreneur (carpet remnant salesman). Lives in beautiful two-bedroom apartment (with parents). Enjoys people (people who talk to jelly). Cleanliness a priority, germ-free a must (repetitive hand washing followed by many scalding showers). Loves to perform (in Mommy and Daddy's room until he's sent to his room)." As accurate as this account is, I don't believe my parents saw me this way because I never received anything but unconditional love and support from them.

It was now 1978. My father had opened the lighting company, and I was working along with him. Terry had finished high school and was working at a textile supply company. Every night after work, we would meet up and hang with some friends who included Terry's sister, Fay, her husband at the time, and their friends. On one particular night after making a spectacle of myself (as usual), Fay's friend Reenie said, "You're really funny, you should go to Yuk Yuk's." That didn't even sound like a sentence to me. What is a Yuk Yuk? Today, Yuk Yuk's, HaHa's, and the Funny Bone all make sense to people as names of comedy clubs, but at that time I didn't know what a comedy club was.

The following night, we made plans and went downtown to this new, hot, bustling club Yuk Yuk's. It was located in something of a strip mall on the corner of Yorkville and Bay streets. When I was a child, my dad would load my family into the car and make an evening of driving up and down Yorkville looking at the hippies. This was essentially our Greenwich Village. By the late 1970s, the hippies had been replaced by upscale restaurants. Yorkville was like a nightlife mecca. And for a kid from the suburbs, it made you feel you had arrived in the big city.

We waited in line, paid the admission, and sat in our seats. The lights went down, a fanfare of music pumped through the room, and Mark Breslin, the owner/master of ceremonies of the proceedings, made his way to the stage. Mark had started the club in the basement of a church in 1975 and then moved it to Bay Street in 1978. He was *the* king of comedy in Toronto. Adding to the excitement, this was the first time I was seeing somebody in person whose picture had been in the paper.

I had never witnessed anything like this in my life. He was funny, irreverent, and edgy. Throughout the night, he brought on a veritable cornucopia of comics, each being as funny and subversive as the last.

At the end of the evening, Mark retook the stage and announced that on the following Wednesday night after the show, there would be a time reserved for amateurs, when anyone could get up and showcase their comedic wares. Everybody at my table turned to me and said, "Howie, you should do it." Without a thought or even a breath, I said, "Let's do it."

My destiny was set.

I had no—absolutely no—concept of what was involved in preparing for this appearance. I had never even prepared for the performances in my parents' room. The fact that somebody had set a date and said show up at this time and be funny caused a terror I had never previously felt. All the pranks and jokes that I had pulled until that point were impulsive. Wednesday night had to be a planned performance.

Adding to my horror, my radar had been enacted. In the days leading up to that Wednesday, I was watching Johnny Carson, Merv Griffin, and Mike Douglas on TV, as I had before. But now I became aware of the stand-ups. I was always aware that they existed, but I had never focused on them. I heard Johnny Carson introduce a comedian who had been plucked from a place called the Comedy Store, which was exactly what Yuk Yuk's was. In our local paper, I noticed an article featuring the faces and talent of the people I had just seen at Yuk Yuk's. This world had always existed, but I had never noticed it. I began to feel the gravity of the situation.

It was April 19, 1978. Yes, the day James Franco was born. I don't even know why I know that, but that was my debut as a comedian. Terry has always kept a scrapbook. One of the things she pasted in it was my horoscope for that day, which read: "Tonight your life will change forever."

We arrived at the club early to see the main show. Since I had signed up to perform, I didn't have to pay admission. That alone was a huge event in my life. I had never gotten into any place for free. The terror rose. They must want something in return. I sat with my friends in the audience and watched the comics. I began to wonder how in the world I could come close to eliciting the response received by the acts we were watching. I excused myself. I thought it would be best if I prepared mentally. I don't know what that means, but that's what I was thinking. To this day, I don't know what preparing mentally means. Let me be honest: I don't believe I'm mentally prepared to write this book.

I made my way backstage. The first person I bumped into

was Louis Dinopoulos, who had changed his name to Lou Dinos for show business seven days earlier. He explained to me that he had gone on amateur night the week before and had been asked back. Wow, this guy was a pro. I was very impressed. He was a warm, friendly guy who took me backstage and showed me the ropes. There were no actual ropes, but he showed me three critical things. Number one, the room where comics hung out and entered the stage. Number two, the kitchen, where you could get free fountain drinks or anatomically correct gingerbread men. And number three . . . I'll be honest with you, this was April 19, 1978, and I don't remember the third thing.

While the show was going on, Lou was introducing me to all the other amateurs who were going to appear. I was fascinated by the fact that there were other people who were willing to put themselves in this position. Before I knew it, my time had come. The professionals had finished, and Mark was introducing the amateurs one by one. We were each given five minutes to shine.

As much as I always wanted to be funny and be accepted, there was never a time or a place for my humor. Whether it was making a spectacle of myself in a classroom or being crude in public, the funny came out of the fact that the time or place was inappropriate. Now I was being called upon to create humor in the most appropriate of places at a designated time.

I heard Mark Breslin announce the most terrifying five words: "Ladies and gentlemen, Howie Mandel."

I made my way toward the stage. I passed through a dark

hallway to a curtain. The audience response to my introduction died down rather quickly, though I could still hear the overenthusiastic table of my friends. Having never been on a stage before, I felt very uncomfortable standing there.

I remember seeing interrogation scenes in movies. The Nazis would tie their victim to a chair in the center of a dark room. There always seemed to be a single light thrust upon the victim, which apparently was the main tool in extracting secrets. I never fully understood that concept until the moment the spotlight at Yuk Yuk's hit my face. All I could see were the eyes in the first row, and they seemed to be saying, "You vill now tell us za secret, Jew boy."

I began to laugh nervously. This was somehow contagious, and the audience members began to giggle with me. My fear turned into self-consciousness as I extended my hand toward the audience and asked, "What? What?" I actually meant, "What are you laughing at?" The more I asked, the more they laughed. The actual secret, which was never revealed, was that I didn't have an act.

The Bobby voice suddenly came to mind, and I made that funny little sound I had showcased in class and my parents' room. I had the little boy spew foul and filthy dialogue. This seemed to bring even more laughter, to which I responded, "What? What?" Until lo and behold, a light came on signaling my time was up.

I promise you, I had done absolutely nothing. But I received a great response. Laughter was like a warm blanket enveloping me and injecting me with a druglike euphoria. Just like sex, this first time was a once-in-a-lifetime experience that I will never forget. As I said good night and proceeded to leave the stage, Mark Breslin passed me, looked me in the eye, and said, "Stick around, we'll talk."

I walked out of the spotlight back into the real world to rejoin Lou Dinos and the rest of the comics. At the end of the show, Mark came back and told me that he thought what I had done was very good—and he would like me to come back next week to do it again. To which I said, "Sure."

I was overwhelmed. I ran to the front of the house, found Terry and my friends, and couldn't wait to share my good fortune. He wanted me to do it *again.* I didn't know what *it* was, but he'd invited me to do *it* again. That night, on that stage, at that moment, I became addicted.

I couldn't wait for the next week. I was totally consumed. I started showing up every single night just to be part of that world. I hung out with Terry, Lou Dinos, and the other comics, watching the shows, sharing funny stories, eating gingerbread, and, like a sponge, soaking up the intricacies of this newfound craft.

This wonderful place was very different from anywhere I had ever been. For the first time it clicked: there were other people like me. Lou Dinos had told me that during the day he was working in a warehouse and was constantly in trouble because his sense of humor was misunderstood. Most of these people spent their time trying to think of funny stories or putting on goofy hats and standing in front of strangers hoping to be accepted and loved. They were outcasts like me.

While most people in the 1970s were going to discos, this was a nightclub for misfits who weren't into dancing. Most of us had day jobs and looked at these nighttime experiences as a fun diversion. This was not considered a career path. It was like playing pickup basketball with your friends. Just because you can't wait for that game each and every Wednesday does not mean you are so delusional as to believe that you will one day play in the NBA.

Mark Breslin's invitation to come back lit a fire in me the likes of which I had never experienced. Years later, I was to meet a phenomenally entertaining artist by the name of Denny Dent, who taught me one of my most significant life lessons: Your happiness lies in finding your passion. He conveyed this message in a unique way. In front of an audience of thousands, he would blast a rock song and paint a wall-size intricate portrait of the artist whose music you were hearing. Before your very eyes, as the song crescendoed and came to an end, he would step back and reveal his completed masterpiece. As his career blossomed, he would use his performance to deliver a motivational message.

Through our friendship, I found out that Denny had gone through a very dark period in his life. He never set out to be a two-fisted musical speed painter. It just so happened that at one of the lowest moments in his life, he threw caution to the wind, blasted on a boom box, and began throwing paint. Within minutes, to his own dismay, he had actually created an amazing image. It wasn't anything he had planned or even knew he had in him. This find turned out to be his calling. He ended up making a great living, raising millions for charity, and motivating countless conventionally thinking people.

His ultimate message in life was that we are all artists regardless of what we do. If we could just throw caution to the wind and be more passionate without giving any thought to the ramifications of our actions, or where they might lead us, chances are we could create something special. A computer programmer may end up with a program the likes of which has never been seen—Microsoft. Somebody who is innovative and passionate about marketing can end up with the next Pet Rock.

This unleashed creative passion could result in success, but his point was that passion alone is the success. We all need it in our lives. If your job may happen to be cleaning toilets, but if you are passionate about your stamp collection and can't wait to get to it, your life is much richer than that of the CEO who drudges through life without a spark of passion for anything.

This philosophy was the reason Denny and I clicked from the moment we met. It was almost as if he were preaching my life. Without a thought of where it might lead me or what the outcome might be, I had stepped on the stage at Yuk Yuk's. On April 19, 1978, shortly before midnight, I had found my passion.

FIVE

I WILL
SUPPORT HER WITH A
RUBBER
GLOVE

I t was 1979. We were in the middle of a comedy boom. If every major city didn't have a club, I assure you one was about to open. Comedy clubs were exciting places to be. Live stand-up had become the newest, freshest form of entertainment for the young. It seemed to be replacing the disco.

On any given night at Yuk Yuk's, Mark Breslin would host and introduce the lineup of regular, unpaid comedians, followed by the one paid featured act. This comic was either one of the club regulars or a headliner from out of town such as Gilbert Gottfried or Jay Leno. Comedic celebrities like Robin Williams might drop in and surprise the audience.

Mark continually invited me back, and within weeks he moved me into the regular lineup. I was now part of the club and, unbeknownst to me, riding that wave to who knew where.

I believe that everyone who made their way to the stage was there because someone else told them they were funny. It might be just a friend or a relative at the dinner table. No one ever made that decision alone, including me. Once you were there, it would be horrifying to find out that only your friends and relatives shared your humor. I always felt incredibly lucky to get laughs from all the strangers making up the audience. It made me feel as if they were sharing in my sense of humor. There's nothing that can make you feel more naked and vulnerable than revealing your own sense of humor publicly. The sound of laughter coming from strangers is like a warm, fuzzy "ME TOO."

I loved being there. I was comfortably uncomfortable on-stage, and I had found my joy. At the same time, had I done a little self-analysis, I might have asked myself, "Every time I walk onstage, I'm petrified. Why am I doing this?" Yet it was a strange comfort zone. This seemed like an incredible dichotomy. In a quest to be noticed, accepted, and loved by strangers, you set yourself up to be ridiculed or humiliated. Silence alone can be humiliating. But as much as you might think I had chosen comedy, it had chosen me.

At this point, I had been attending this comedy soiree every night for five months. Amazingly, Mark asked me to headline the show. I became the featured act for the week. My name was on the marquee along with the tagline "Borderline Psychotic," a reference to my hyperkinetic nervous energy onstage. But when you come to think about it, that tagline doesn't stray too far from the reality.

Being a featured act was a huge responsibility. I was forced to deliver. I had to do nine shows a week, one each day and two on Friday and Saturday nights. I'd like to thank Terry, who seemed to enjoy these times as much as me. I couldn't believe she would put up with going to a comedy club each and every night. (I still can't.) I remember the time Terry had gotten tickets for us to see George Harrison live. A Beatle was coming to our town, and we had tickets. But I had to inform her that I couldn't make it.

This was going to be my first real job in comedy. This was a feature, and Yuk Yuk's was actually paying me for my services. For the nine shows, I would end up with a check for $150. If you do the math, that comes out to approximately $17 per show. Even though I would miss only one performance to see a Beatle, how could I walk away from $17? The truth is that I couldn't walk away from the stage, and Terry understood that.

When I told her that I couldn't go, I was prepared for her to be upset and at least inflict some guilt on me. She had been spending every single night for the past five months in a comedy club. This was to be her special night out. But instead, she encouraged me to fulfill my obligation. To this day, after thirty-one years of touring and being away from home for weeks at a time, along with countless other obligations, she has given me nothing but support and love, not to mention putting up with the borderline psychotic side of me.

It was so hard to concentrate at work during the day. I was consumed with the preparations involved in being the featured act. Unbelievable as this may sound, it wasn't about the material. It was the fact that I was getting $17 a show. Do you know what kind of pressure that puts on one's shoulders? For the last five months, I had been showing up for free and just trying to be funny. Now I was earning a gazillion percent more. Just the fact that somebody was paying me meant it was a job carrying heavy responsibility.

My act was mostly me just being me. Some people might call that "filler." There was a lot of giggling and me asking, "What? What?" But on the road to becoming a featured act, I had expanded my repertoire. I had created this character called Donny. He was half man, half chicken. I stuffed my cheeks and moved around the stage like a spastic fowl, telling the audience: "Daddy was a lonely chicken farmer. Mommy was a chicken." Then I would reminisce about my childhood when I woke up in the morning and heard Mommy in the kitchen making eggs. I'd then make a grunting sound, as if I were a chicken pushing an egg . . . out of its ass.

I closed the set with the Bobby character. Terry's mom had sewed me a bonnet to wear. I would then drop my pants to reveal towels tucked into my underpants, giving the impression I was wearing a diaper. I immediately launched into a series of filthy observations in that cute little falsetto.

Nothing but brilliance. It was worth every penny of that $17 they paid me. It was so exciting. I thought I had arrived. I was a featured act. I was being paid. I was on the marquee, even though you had to walk downstairs to actually see the marquee. I truly loved being the featured act for that week, and by the way, Terry truly loved the George Harrison concert.

By the following week, life had returned to normal. I continued to hang out at the club every night, doing my comedy sets in the regular lineup.

Life was good. Terry was great, so I decided to take it to the next level. I asked her to marry me. Actually, that sounds a lot more romantic than it was. One night after my set, we went across the street to Meyers Delicatessen. She ordered a corned beef sandwich. I had the pastrami. When the sandwiches arrived, I told her I had to go to the men's room. As I got up from the table, I reached into my pocket, pulled out a diamond my father had helped me purchase, threw it on the table, and said, "If you want to make an engagement ring out of that, let me know. I'll be right back, I gotta piss." I don't know why Hallmark never hired me.

As crass as this may sound, I want you to know that Terry is one of the least romantic people I've ever met, so as unromantic as this sounds, it happens to be who we are. Over the past thirty years, I've brought home flowers once. Her response was "Who gave you these?" You would think her response to this landmark gesture would've been, "Wow, how romantic, these are beautiful." Truth be told, they were given to me by the set decorator on *St. Elsewhere*, who was going to throw them out anyway. Terry knows me too well.

In 1979, I decided to take a week off work and visit Los Angeles, for no other reason than it sounded like a great vacation. I had never been anywhere but Toronto and Miami.

Our tour group consisted of me, Terry, Lou Dinos, and

two of our noncomedy friends, Jeff Weiman and Cindy Kleinberg. We landed in sunny Southern California, which seemed so culturally different from anything I had ever experienced. This trip was supposed to be a once-in-a-lifetime sightseeing vacation. As I sit here thirty years later, I feel like Gilligan. In 1979, I was embarking on what was supposed to be my three-hour tour. Yet here I am marooned in the midst of a beautiful life and unbelievable career. You have no idea how far this is from what I ever dreamed I would be doing. I'd always figured that if I were ever lucky enough to be writing a book at this stage of my life, chapter 5 would likely focus on the wearability of shag carpet.

One of the top tourist destinations in Los Angeles was the world-famous Comedy Store. It seemed that everybody who was anybody in comedy was being discovered there: Freddie Prinze from *Chico and the Man*, Jimmie Walker from *Good Times*, and Robin Williams of *Mork & Mindy*.

As luck would have it, the night we happened on the Comedy Store was amateur night, which featured lesser-known comedians. I saw people outside I recognized. One of these was Mike Binder, a young comedian from Detroit whom I had met at Yuk Yuk's. He was now living in Los Angeles and told me that he was a regular on a comedy game show called *Make Me Laugh*.

This was a half-hour syndicated show that did not air in Canada. It was hosted by Bobby Van and featured three comedians who would be on every night for an entire week. Each comedian would take a minute to entertain a contestant. The challenge was to not laugh. For every minute they didn't laugh, the contestants would win money. As if comedy is not hard enough, why not perform for people who are paid not to laugh? That being said, it was a hugely entertaining show.

Mike told me about the show and introduced me to the executive producer, George Foster, who also happened to be there that night. Mike knew the ropes at the Comedy Store, so he helped me sign up for a set. I just thought of this as another fun moment in my vacation. In no way was I aspiring to move my career along. I don't think that I was aware there was a career to be had.

After regaling the American audience with my five-minute Yuk Yuk's routine, Mike told me that George Foster thought I was a good candidate for *Make Me Laugh.* I was invited to his office the next day. This trip was turning out to be much more than I had envisioned.

The next day I showed up at the gates of KTLA, an independent local TV station that was also the locale for numerous TV productions. I had been on the Universal Studios tour, where I don't believe I got anywhere near real show business. The closest I had gotten was a plastic-looking shark jumping out of a lagoon and splashing our tram. Here there were no tours, just giant warehouses filled with people making television shows. When I got to George's office, he told me that I was very funny and ordered me to make his secretary laugh. I can't remember what I did, but apparently it was worthy of being invited to appear on the show.

I was asked to make myself available for one day. The show taped five episodes in a day, which aired over the course of a week. I flew home and had a great story to tell about my vacation.

At this point, my father and I were in the lighting business together. The company had expanded to the point where we had a very nice downtown office and a sales staff of fifteen, including Lou Dinos.

One day at the office, I got a call at three in the afternoon asking if I was available to do an impromptu show at seven that same night. Without hesitation, I said yes. I had committed. I asked for directions to the club. And then came the details.

It was not going to be at a club. The venue would be slightly bigger. I was to perform at Maple Leaf Gardens, Toronto's largest indoor arena, and be the opener for Earth, Wind & Fire's sold-out concert. As I listened to the details, I was sure somebody had to be playing a joke on me. This was 1979, and I was not that well-known. But as it turned out, I was what the promoters needed.

A few weeks earlier at a concert for the Who, eleven fans had been trampled to death in Cincinnati. The papers attributed the tragedy to crowd mismanagement. The promoter had just realized that Earth, Wind & Fire's production setup was running behind schedule. Rather than pushing the show back a half hour and holding the huge crowd outside, risking a repeat of what had happened in Cincinnati, they came up with the brilliant idea of putting a comedian on the stage. The comedian would perform as they continued to complete the setup.

They explained the procedure for the show to me. The lights would go down, and I would take the stage. Behind me in the darkness, the crew would continue the final preparations for the show. They would then signal me that the band was ready to play, and I would wrap up.

I thought, Maple Leaf Gardens! That's where the Toronto Maple Leafs play. This is my hometown. I excitedly called Terry. She and a group of our friends came down. The entire experience was surreal.

I had to finish my work at the office first, so I arrived backstage just minutes before the show. I had hoped to meet Earth, Wind & Fire, but there was no time. As the lights went down, I heard the deafening roar of fifteen thousand people. It seemed as if the voice of God came over the PA system and announced, "Before Earth, Wind and Fire takes the stage, please welcome local comedian Howie Mandel!"

The roar dulled, but it still remained louder than anything I had ever heard for me. As I walked onto the giant stage, I was blinded by a spotlight. I looked out into an endless abyss of darkness and began my act. I don't remember the specifics, but it was not going over that well. So like most young, inexperienced comics when the going gets tough, I went for the filth. I started using the f-word. The laughs came. These were young concertgoers. The laughter began to build. Not that I was particularly funny—they were responding to the vulgarity alone.

My confidence returned. I veered back into my regular routine. Once again, I could hear the roar of fifteen thousand people. I had them in the palm of my hand. As I finished one particular piece, I noticed I didn't get a response. I moved on. In the midst of the next piece, I began to feel the audience wasn't listening to me. They began chanting, "Earth, Wind and Fire! Earth, Wind and Fire!" I had lost them. It was as if I weren't even there. I figured if you can't beat 'em, join 'em, so I chanted, "Earth, Wind and Fire!"

When I was six months old, the only thing coming between me and the world was plastic. To you it's just a sheet of plastic; to me it's my destiny.

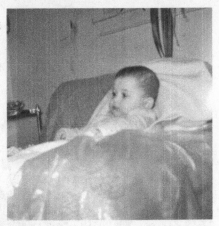

This is me at four years old with "the baby" in the cage behind me.

My prizewinning smile on the vacation in Miami during which I was bitten by a sand fly.

I think Mom and Dad wanted my brother Steve and me either to be flight attendants or to work for Century 21. Early 1960s.

At fifteen, I always overdressed for picture day.

The most amazing couple ever, my parents, Al and Evy Mandel.

I don't know if this is me at my bar mitzvah or just a Canadian Jew wearing a hat and scarf.

This is Terry, the beauty I finally convinced to go out with me. You can see the excitement in her face.

April 19, 1978. Yuk Yuk's, Toronto, Canada. My very first performance ever on my way to becoming an author.

My first marquee, for my first real job in comedy, September 1979.

Backstage at Yuk Yuk's minutes before I took the stage for my first paid gig.

Working toward my $150 doing Donny the half man, half chicken at Yuk Yuk's during my feature.

Left: A rubber glove, a handbag, a career, sometime in 1982.

Below left: My first night at Caesars Palace opening for Diana Ross. I'm standing in a paper bag doing my impression of groceries, and contemplating the silence.

Below right: Doing what I believe is my big closing. About to find out it's not over.

Mid-1980s at the Bismarck Theatre in Chicago, shooting my North American Watusi Tour for HBO.

My very first billboard on Sunset Boulevard, 1984. A star is born.

Look, Mom, I am a *doctor*! (Some of the cast, clockwise from top left: William Daniels, Ed Flanders, Denzel Washington, Ed Begley Jr., David Morse, Ellen Bry, Cynthia Sykes and *moi*.)

I always wanted a mustache, but not under my nose. It's real, folks. I kept it for three months.

On the set of *A Fine Mess*, being regaled with stories from the legendary Blake Edwards.

I looked over to my left, and there was a stagehand frantically motioning me over to him. I couldn't just walk off in front of fifteen thousand people in the middle of a routine. Then it hit me. This must be my signal that they were ready. This had to be the moment I was supposed to introduce Earth, Wind & Fire.

So I quickly segued to my closing, throughout which the audience continued to chant. With a combination of relief and excitement, I screamed into the microphone, "Ladies and gentlemen, enjoy Earth, Wind and Fire!" No one even flinched. They just continued chanting, "Earth, Wind and Fire!"

I ran offstage, confused. The stagehand ushered me through the backstage hallways to a hockey dressing room. He told me to wait there and then slammed the door behind me.

I waited for a few moments. Finally, I tried to open the door. It was locked. I started to panic. I had no idea what had happened. I was just onstage a minute ago, and now I was locked in a hockey dressing room. I could hear the entire Maple Leaf Gardens arena reverberating with the chant "Earth, Wind and Fire!"

As I was banging on the door, trying to get out, a booming announcement began: "Ladies and gentlemen, can I have your attention. Earth, Wind and Fire would like to separate themselves from the vulgarity of the opening act, so the concert will be delayed by twenty minutes."

I was in a state of shock. I was banging and kicking against the door. It was as if I were trapped in an insane asylum. I wanted to run out there and trample eleven people. After the announcement, one of the crew members unlocked the door. I found Terry and ran home in a haze of public humiliation.

I realized that if I'd had a chance to meet Earth, Wind & Fire, none of this would've happened. Apparently, at this time they were very spiritual and religious. One of the reasons they were unavailable to meet me was that they were in a room praying. I found out that as soon as my first vulgarity was uttered, production was instructed to pull the plug on the microphone. When I spoke into the mike, I could hear my voice through a small monitor at my feet. I had no sense of how it sounded in the arena. I now realized how I had gone from fifteen thousand people loving me and laughing with me to being so completely turned off. It wasn't the audience who was turned off; it was the sound. Hence they began to chant. I was disgraced and hung out to dry in my own hometown. As devastating as this may sound, I took solace in the fact that I had played the stage at Maple Leaf Gardens, and I was indeed in show business.

In hindsight, I believe this was God's way of giving me a taste of my own medicine. I can't remember any other time in my life when someone wanted to be separated from me because I was the dirty one.

Within a few weeks, I got a call from NBC. They said Dick Shawn had seen me on *Make Me Laugh* and wanted to use me for his pilot. I told them I knew nothing about planes and was embarrassed to find out "pilot" was the term for a test episode of a new TV series. I happened to be a big fan. He was great in the movie *The Producers* as Hitler in the play within the movie. His stand-up was also legendary.

Without hesitation, I told my dad I would have to take more time off and fly back to L.A. Again, I assure you I just considered this a happening. I will admit I found it really cool to be able to tell everyone, "I have to fly to L.A." I had never met someone who had to be in L.A. for anything.

Not long after that, I got a call from *The Mike Douglas Show*. The booker there had also seen *Make Me Laugh* and wanted me to appear on his show. This call was even more thrilling because I had watched Mike Douglas's talk show every day of my life. He was one of the early pioneers of daytime talk shows. One week, John Lennon and Yoko Ono had co-hosted with Mike. It seemed surreal. I again told my father, "I have to fly to L.A." The guests on that episode were Bobby Vinton, Adolfo "Shabba-Doo" Quinones, who would go on to star in a movie called *Breakin' 2: Electric Boogaloo*, a singing bird, and a twenty-three-year-old engaged lighting salesman living with his parents in Toronto, Canada, by the name of Howie Mandel.

My stage act was expanding. One night, because I had nothing else to do—yet another blank moment of terror onstage—I pulled out a rubber glove I carried for germ protection and thought, I'll pull it over my head.

At first, I did a rooster impression. The audience laughed. I then pulled the glove even farther down below my eyebrows and over my nose. As I was breathing through my nose, the fingers were going up and down. More laughter. Next, I decided to exhale through my nose and inflate the glove until it popped. The audience roared. I thought, Oh, my gosh, I have a new closing.

For years after that, I was known as "the guy who put the rubber glove on his head." There was no talent involved, but people would still request it. They'd yell, "Do the glove!" It became my signature piece.

What I have come to realize is that you can't decide something will be your signature piece. You just do something, and it becomes your signature. The things that you become known for and the things that bring the biggest response can't be planned.

Not too long after that appearance, Alan Thicke called and asked me to come and tape many segments on his new nighttime variety show in Vancouver. Alan's show segued into *Thicke of the Night* for American consumption, and eventually he starred in *Growing Pains,* which you all remember I was never a part of. I returned to my father's office and told him once again, "I have to fly to L.A." I just thought that sounded better than Vancouver.

For all these appearances, I was being paid what is known in the business as "scale." Scale in show business is considered minimum wage, but I can assure you that scale is nowhere near real minimum wage. For an appearance on a show like *Mike Douglas,* acting silly for a couple of minutes and answering two or three questions, I was paid something like $300. At Yuk Yuk's, I had to do eighteen shows to earn that kind of money.

So here's how my mind worked. If I am constantly being called and asked to spend a few minutes with people for $300, can you imagine how much I would make if I decided to do this full-time? I'm young. I have my whole life ahead of me. I can always rejoin my father's business. I've got nothing to lose.

I remember heading into my father's office, saying, "Dad—"

"Don't tell me," he interrupted me. "You have to fly to L.A."

"Yes, but this time it's different," I said.

"Why?" he asked.

"Because I'm not coming back."

I don't think he said anything, but then again what could he say? He would never tell me not to go. He would never say that it was a crazy idea. Like my mother, he would only support me and love me unconditionally. That had always been my parents' way.

Now, I don't know if you remember this, but I happened to be engaged, and there was a wedding being planned for March 16, 1980, by the bride's family. I've never been one for etiquette, but I think it's customary for the groom to inform the future in-laws that he will be quitting his job and moving their daughter to California.

Terry's parents were horrified. I thought their fears were ridiculous. Now that I'm a parent of two daughters, I understand. But at that time, most people growing up in suburban Toronto never moved out of town even for college, much less to Los Angeles without a job. My basic pitch to them was: "Here's what I'm going to do. I'm going to take your daughter two thousand miles away to another culture and try to care for her by putting a rubber glove on my head. Don't worry." This sounded great to me, and this also ensured that our wedding would have out-of-town guests: us.

December 15, 1979, was the date that Terry and I moved permanently to Los Angeles. I quickly learned that jobs weren't as easy to come by as those random phone calls I was receiving in Toronto. I would do odd sets here and there for $50 or $75. We virtually lived off of our savings.

As for accommodations, we made a deal with the manager of the Holiday Inn at the corner of Hollywood Boulevard and Highland. The roof of the hotel had a revolving restaurant with a view of the entire city. Traditionally, revolving restaurants are propelled by a huge, noisy motor. I know this because for a very good price we were given the room with the motor. Needless to say, that didn't last very long. After a few pit stops, we ended up with a quaint apartment in Studio City. We bought a hibachi and fed ourselves cheaply most nights. If we wanted to splurge once a week, we could afford to go to Art's Deli and split a double-decker sandwich.

There are no words to describe how exciting that time was for both of us. We were living in California. For the first time, we had our own place. And we were hanging out at the Comedy Store every night.

Before we knew it, March 16 had arrived. We flew to Toronto on an overdrawn credit card to attend our wedding. Luckily, our parents had asked most of the guests to give us cash in lieu of gifts, so we were able to repay our credit card and retain some savings.

I had a lot of fun at my own wedding. I wore a top hat and tails and carried a white cane. I remember coming down the aisle tapping that cane as if I were blind, mumbling to guests in the sanctuary, "Can anybody see her? Is she pretty?"

During the ceremony, the rabbi asked me to repeat after him: "I take Terry . . ." I repeated, "You take Terry . . ." He said, "No, you take Terry." I said, "Forget it, you take her." The rabbi did not find me funny.

The evening turned out to be one of the highlights and best decisions I made in my life. The honeymoon, not so much. I just outlined my financial circumstances, so you will be able to understand. Before we flew in, I had negotiated a deal with Mark Breslin in order to make this wedding trip a twofer. I would fly in for the wedding, therefore he would not have to pay for my travel, as he did for other out-of-town acts, and I would be a featured headliner at Yuk Yuk's for three nights.

From a business standpoint, this was a very good deal. Personally, not so much. The night following my wedding, I was performing on the stage at Yuk Yuk's—with my bride on a stool next to me. I informed the audience that I had gotten married the previous night and they were all taking part in our honeymoon. In subsequent years, we have traveled and seen the world but have never actually gone on a designated honeymoon. I'll let you in on a little secret: I have decided to bring Terry on the book tour to promote this book as a second honeymoon.

So here's how the story goes up until now. Boy meets girl. Boy finds comedy. Boy brings girl to comedy club. Boy marries girl. Boy brings girl back to comedy club for honeymoon. Boy and girl move on to new chapter.

SIX

A DRAMATIC TURN OF EVENTS

Up until this point, I had been a guy who did comedy—but now I was a *comedian*. An unemployed comedian. An unemployed comedian with a wife, who was also unemployed. An unemployed comedian with an unemployed wife living off of our wedding cash. To those people who didn't receive thank-you notes, I can't tell you how grateful I am for your contribution.

Our whole life became centered around the Comedy Store. This was the mecca. Anybody who was anyone in show business was either in the audience or performing. This was the place to be and be seen. The caliber of comedy was top-notch. On any given night, the lineup could've included Steve Martin, Billy Crystal, Robin Williams, or Rodney Danger-field working out his *Tonight Show* routine. The MC might've been an up-and-coming comedian by the name of David Letterman. There was always a huge crowd lined up along the Sunset Strip waiting to get in. Being part of this was not only exciting, it changed how I approached comedy.

Richard Pryor had also been showing up nightly to hone his act before filming his concert movie *Live on the Sunset Strip*. It was amazing to watch him create something from nothing. On one particular night, I believe I witnessed the epitome of brilliance. I can't remember the exact wording of the routine, and I'm not going to do it justice, but it had a profound impact on me.

Pryor is onstage portraying himself as the Lord. The audience is responding with convulsive, euphoric laughter. He then tells the audience that he has to leave and get back to doing the Lord's work. He's down here only to pick up his son. The laughter continues, and so does Richard.

"Where is my son?" he asks, looking out into the audience. "Have you seen him? He's a young Jewish-looking boy with long hair and a beard. Has anybody seen Jesus?" He pauses and waits for an answer from the audience.

The laughter begins to die down. Everyone is waiting to see where this is going. Then he listens, as though someone is answering him silently. A look of horror appears on his face. A long, uncomfortable pause as realization sets in.

"What the fuck did you do with my son?" He pauses. "You did what?" His eyes start to fill with tears, and he starts to scream in pain, "How the fuck could you do that? That's my son, that's my baby. That's my boy. What the fuck is wrong with you people?"

He then gathers himself and says, "All right, I need to talk to Saint Peter. Bring him here now. Where is he?" The laughter is now completely gone. His eyes widen. As if in total disbelief, he says, "Him too?" Pause. Then with painful resolve, he says, "Okay, then I need to talk to Martin Luther King." Pause. "Where's Dr. King? What? . . . When? . . . Are you fucking kidding me?"

Tears are now running down his cheeks. As he seems to be physically writhing in agony, he turns his back to the audience. The tension in the room builds. He slowly turns back to face us as he implores us to bring him John F. Kennedy. Pause. He looks at us and screams, "How could you? No! No!" Then silence. Then tears.

His eyes look like daggers piercing each and every audience member. He sweeps his arms, pointing at everybody in the audience as if he were accusing each and every one of us. Through his tears, he says, "You're on your own." And he walks off the stage, down the center aisle, and out of that room in silence.

Everyone sat there emotionally paralyzed. They had just been confronted with the reality that humanity has been destroying itself. Within the span of five minutes, we had gone from the heights of convulsive laughter to the depths of dark despair—and he had controlled that. It was the most brilliant moment I had ever seen in performance.

That night changed my approach to performing. Aside from being emotionally moving, what Pryor had done was incredibly brave. It was unheard of in the world of comedy to try to elicit anything but laughter. Even if it was thought-provoking, it was usually laughter just the same. To go up onstage and share an incredibly dark truth and elicit tears goes far beyond the realm of comedy. That bravery inspires me to this day to push my own comedic envelope. That being said, I don't believe I have the capacity ever to create anything even close to the brilliance of Richard Pryor.

I was now hanging in this world among the great and soon-to-be-great comedians. As fun as this place was to be, it wasn't very warm. Each comedian was vying for his own moment in the sun. The only person who ever talked to me was Jay Leno, whom I'd met at Yuk Yuk's. He would provide me with transportation. Can you believe it, Jay Leno actually had a car. He would pick me up and take me to other clubs, where we would do our acts. He's always been a good, down-to-earth guy and remains that same person today.

Each week was devoted to landing spots at the club. You would call the Comedy Store on Monday with your availabilities. Getting a spot was intensely competitive. You would then call back on Tuesday morning to find out the days and times of your spots. Landing each spot was like winning the lottery.

I would usually end up with about five spots for the week. I always hoped one would be on a Thursday night, when producers and casting directors from the various networks and shows would be in the audience to handpick talent. Just about every job I got at that time, such as *Norm Crosby's Comedy Shop,* Showtime's *Laugh-a-thon,* and *The Merv Griffin Show,* was from being seen on Thursday.

I operated like an entrepreneur. I realized more than anything this was a business. If I was booked on a show, I would send out flyers to the casting people to make sure they tuned in. The call from *Merv Griffin* came in at two in the afternoon for a four o'clock taping that same day. I (almost) didn't want to do it, because I wouldn't have time to publicize my appearance before the show aired the following day. There was no time to take out a small ad in *Variety*, and I was upset that my name wouldn't be in *TV Guide*. This was way before TiVo, so I was afraid nobody in the business would see me. It was still very exciting for me to be appearing on *Merv Griffin* and working with the lead guest, Desi Arnaz, who'd played Ricky on *I Love Lucy*.

Terry and I called Toronto and told our parents to watch. As soon as the show aired, my parents called and told me how proud they were. Terry's parents didn't call. They didn't call the following day, either. Finally she called them, but they didn't mention the show.

At last Terry asked, "Did you see Howie on *Merv Griffin*?"

"Yes," her mother replied. "So what happened?"

"What do you mean?" Terry said.

"Well, we turned it on the next day, and he was gone . . . he got fired, didn't he?" she said.

It took them a while to grasp this whole show business deal.

Gene Simmons from the rock band Kiss had also seen the show. His girlfriend at the time was Diana Ross. He liked me so much, he apparently suggested Diana book me as her opening act at Caesars Palace in Las Vegas. When my agent gave me the news, I couldn't believe my luck.

Now, at that point I didn't really have much of an act. I did some characters, had a few funny voices, and used the rubber glove as a closing. I certainly didn't have a polished half hour worthy of Las Vegas. I was this kid from Toronto who had never seen Vegas.

As soon as I arrived at Caesars Palace, I found my way backstage. I felt as if I had been dropped into a palatial Roman scene from *Ben-Hur*. I had performed at Yuk Yuk's and the Comedy Store. Now I was going to be with Diana Ross at Circus Maximus. This was a whole new world.

The guard asked who I was, and I told him I was Diana Ross's opening act. I could hardly believe I said that. He told me that he had a dressing room ready for me. I had never had a dressing room. I had been locked in a dressing room at Maple Leaf Gardens, but that is totally different. As we approached the door, I could see a gold placard with my name: Howie Mandell. I told the guard, "Mandel is not spelled with two *l*'s." When he asked me how many it was supposed to be, I told him six. He looked at me confused and turned away. I could feel my humor was really clicking here.

I walked in, and he closed the door behind me. It was a very fancy room with a baby grand piano, a full bar, and a table of snacks. It looked like a place the Rat Pack would hang out in before a show. I thought I must be in the wrong room. Maybe there was a Howie Mandell with two *l*'s who deserved this. I didn't know what to do. I ate a celery stick.

I had gotten dressed in my hotel room in what I thought a Vegas showman would wear. I had flamboyantly horrible, bright red pants, a very sparkly tie, and a beige sports jacket from my engagement party. On the lapel of the jacket, I had clipped a giant rubber alligator I had bought at a novelty store to depict the Lacoste style.

There was a knock at the door, and when I answered it, it was the same guy. "You know what you have to do tonight?" he asked.

"Yes, I'm opening for Diana Ross," I replied.

"You have to do thirty minutes, okay?" he said forcefully.

"Okay," I assured him.

"So you understand what I'm telling you," he continued. Why was he repeating himself?

"I'm telling you, thirty minutes," he persisted. "Not twenty-nine. Not thirty-one. Thirty minutes."

"I don't wear a watch, so can you signal me at twenty-nine minutes by just banging your foot on the floor behind me?" I figured that putting the glove over my head, blowing it up, and popping it off would take about a minute. He agreed, and I gave him a few bucks for his trouble.

I should explain that the reason I had to do thirty minutes and not twenty-nine is that the show was perfectly timed. Casinos make money by having people on the gambling floor. If a show started at nine p.m., they wanted the audience out by ten-thirty sharp. Every minute the customers spent watching a show, they were not dropping money in the casino. Diana Ross also had everything perfectly timed. She needed to walk out of her dressing room and onto the stage precisely at nine-thirty.

Because she had an elaborate stage setup with a full orchestra and backup singers, I worked in front of the curtain on a three-foot lip of stage. They had a stand-up microphone, which I couldn't move. It literally felt as if I were standing on the edge of a cliff.

I was really nervous the first night. I felt so far out of my league. I kept thinking that I didn't deserve to be there, and I probably didn't. Whose idea was this, anyway? Right, the fire-breathing lead singer of Kiss.

The lights went down. The audience roared in anticipation. And then an ominous, baritone voice came over the PA system: "Ladies and gentlemen, Caesars Palace is proud to present an evening with Diana Ross!" The crowd exploded. If you listened really closely—and there's no reason why anyone but me would—you could also hear, ". . . andspecialguesthowiemandel."

The crowd was under the impression that they were going to be presented with Diana Ross, but instead this little Jew wandered out from stage left. I stood there frozen in place. People were looking at me like, "Who the hell are you? What are you doing here?" It was as if I came out of the restroom and took a wrong turn. This wasn't a welcoming crowd.

I bade everyone good evening, and then I went into my act. I told the first joke, which I had done on *Merv Griffin* . . . silence. I tried a few more . . . silence. I remember one particular bit when I said, "Now I will do my impression of groceries." I took out a shopping bag and proceeded to stand in it . . . silence for an inordinate amount of time. Get it? Neither did they.

This brings back a particular childhood memory. Every Sunday throughout my childhood, I went to visit my grandparents on my mother's side for dinner. They were my zaidi and my bubbie. Zaidi was a dry cleaner and tailor and a perfectionist. I can't tell you how many times I showed up wearing a pair of pants he felt needed an upgrade. He'd scream at me to take them off. "They must be fixed now!" I would have to stand there in front of everyone at the dinner table and remove my pants. There I sat, eating my chicken in silence, wearing my tighty-whities while he repaired the flaw. It was always a painfully awkward and uncomfortable silence—not unlike the silence from the Caesars audience.

Their silence began to turn to anger. The feeling was "Enough of this. We paid to see Diana Ross. Why the hell is this guy wasting our time?"

The audience was right there at my feet. In fact, one lady in the first row took her fist, banged on my toe, and said, "Get the fuck off the stage."

I didn't answer her. This obviously wasn't my audience. I just ignored it and let my toes go numb. I started to feel at home. When I say "at home," I mean at my performance opening up for Earth, Wind & Fire, or at least as if I was eating chicken in my underpants.

I continued going through whatever I had planned—all of which was met by silence. No matter what I said, there was no response. I began to sweat through my sports coat. Finally, after what seemed like an hour and a half, came the best sound I have ever heard in my life—a *stomp, stomp* from behind the curtain. I thought, This is my savior. I took out the glove, put it on my head, and inflated it. There was not a sound from the audience. As much as it felt bad to say something and not get a response, the commitment of taking out a latex glove, pulling it over your head, and inflating it to silence was torture.

Inside the glove, I was trying to be the consummate optimist. I thought, This is probably double-thick latex, and maybe they're roaring. For the dramatic closing, I let the glove pop off my head. My hands were outstretched. The glove fluttered and landed at my feet . . . silence.

Then I said: "And now, ladies and gentlemen, please enjoy Miss Diana Ross!" The crowd went nuts. I turned around and looked for the opening in the curtain, but I couldn't find it. I began feeling desperately along the curtain to find the crack so I could make my escape. But somebody on the other side was holding it closed.

The crowd was still going nuts anticipating Diana Ross, but the room grew quieter and quieter as I was pleading with someone to let me through the curtain. From the other side, I heard a man's voice saying, "No, no." I'm thinking, What do you mean, no? I'm literally three feet from the audience. The lady who was hitting my foot could hear him.

"What are you doing?" I said.

"You have nine more minutes," he said.

I have nine more minutes! "What are you talking about?"

"You have nine more minutes," he repeated.

I turned around and faced the audience. The room was dead silent. I didn't have nine more minutes. I didn't have the first twenty-one minutes. My ending, the rubber glove, which was usually a big hit, had bombed. I stood up there and treaded for my life for the next nine minutes. I could hear myself swallow. I could hear myself breathe. I could hear my heart banging against my chest. I think I actually heard myself sweating. But there were no other sounds. And then finally I said, "Good night." I swear I heard the audience in unison say, "It's about fucking time." The curtain parted, and I escaped.

What I ended up finding out later was that the band was setting up and I had heard somebody walking by. I'd thought it was the signal. That's how quiet the audience was: I could hear regular footsteps behind me.

A week of hatred passed. I did two shows a night for seven nights. In my book, that's hatred times fourteen. My wife made friends with all the people in the band. She would go on day trips with them to Hoover Dam and Lake Mead. I felt so humiliated, I didn't want to show my face in public. I stayed in my room. I was crazily depressed. The only comfort I could find was in washing my hands and taking countless hot showers.

One particular night, I was told they were renting out the theater to Sony Japan. The entire room was full of Japanese people. They knew Diana Ross and the Supremes. But before they could hear her, I had to go out and do my act in front of Japanese people who didn't speak English. I'll tell you something, it wasn't any worse.

Midway through the first week, I received a note from Diana Ross that read, "I wish I could come out and see you." I was thinking, I wish she wouldn't. At the end of the week, her people sent word that she wanted to see me in her dressing room before the show. Ah, I've seen this trick before. They aren't going to be there, and they are just going to lock me in. Or if she is there, I'm fired. Thank God it's over.

I walked to her dressing room and knocked on the door. I heard her voice say, "Come on in." She was sitting on the couch in her pre-show outfit. She truly looked like, and was, a superstar. This was my first personal encounter with an entertainment icon. Considering the week I had endured, all I really wanted her to say was "Stop, in the name of love!"

But these were not her words. To this day, I have no idea where she was or what she saw during my shows. But she told me that I was doing very well, she really liked my work, and she had decided to hold me over for another two weeks. Twenty-eight more shows. Twenty-eight more public humiliations. Twenty-eight more half hours of silence.

By the time it was over, I had done a total of three weeks in Las Vegas. The response never got better. It was horrible. Occasionally, I would hear laughter coming from the horn section of the band behind the curtain, but that was it. The audience projected pure hatred. When it was over, I wanted to burn my red pants and sparkly tie.

I had never experienced anything like this before. From the first moment I walked onstage at Yuk Yuk's, I had been accepted by the audience and by Mark Breslin. I had been accepted by the Comedy Store and by George Foster, who booked me on *Make Me Laugh*. Even the Earth, Wind & Fire audience enjoyed what they were able to hear. My every appearance, including *Merv Griffin*, was met with laughter and positive acceptance. Now it felt as if each and every night I was publicly kicked in the nuts and discarded as a useless waste of time.

This was my professional low point. This experience was so painful that I could not see how it would lead to anything positive. I felt so disappointed and depressed that I was sure I wanted to quit. I wanted to go home. I wanted to sell lights with my father. Terry, on the other hand, thought that would be an incredible waste. She believed comedy was my destiny. She encouraged me to go on, though I had no idea what "on" meant.

Obviously, the red pants and sparkly tie weren't working for me. I decided I needed a new uniform. I went out and bought white scrubs—a foreshadowing of things to come. Onstage, the combination of this uniform and my maniacal, kinetic energy gave the audience the impression they were watching a mental patient. Little did they know, they were.

After one Thursday night spot, I was approached by Brenda Carlin, wife of the legendary comic George Carlin. Brenda was a casting director for HBO's *Young Comedians*. I had no idea what HBO was, but I was thrilled to accept the job. The show was taped at the famed Roxy Theatre on the Sunset Strip, hosted by the legendary Smothers Brothers. The special was to present four young, up-and-coming comics. On the bill with me were Richard Lewis, Harry Anderson, and Jerry Seinfeld. You can still see that performance today on YouTube, white scrubs and all. And no, I'm not on cocaine.

This appearance seemed to go fabulously well. It erased the mental stench left by Vegas. I called my agent to ask him what was next. He explained the natural progression for comics at this time was a sitcom. Billy Crystal was on *Soap*. Robin Williams starred in *Mork & Mindy*. Freddie Prinze had *Chico and the Man*. Jimmie Walker was on *Good Times*, and Gabe Kaplan was Kotter. So why not Howie Mandel?

A meeting was set up for me at MTM, which stands for Mary Tyler Moore. After starring in one of the most successful sitcoms ever, Moore and her husband, the highly regarded television programmer Grant Tinker, had formed a company to produce shows. MTM had immediate success with several sitcoms, notably *The Bob Newhart Show, Rhoda*, and *WKRP in Cincinnati*. They also were responsible for the drama *Hill Street Blues*.

I met with Molly Lopata, who did casting for MTM. She asked me if I could act. I told her I thought I could. She asked me to read some pages. I was to read the part of Fiscus. Most of it was highly technical medical terminology and wasn't making a lot of sense to me. Here's an example of what it might have looked like:

NURSE

What do we need, Fiscus?

FISCUS

D-5 Lactated Ringer's, O-negative blood, an intubation tray with two number 16 central intravenous catheters, an open thoracotomy tray, and a MAST suit stat.

Before I could finish, Molly told me I was very good and then brought me into the offices of Bruce Paltrow—who is now best known as Gwyneth's dad but at that time was the headliner in the family. Mark Tinker, who worked with Bruce at MTM, was also there, as were John Falsey and Joshua Brand, whom I learned created the show I was reading for.

I read for them. Halfway through this medical jargon, Bruce stopped me and told me I was very good. He thanked me for coming. There was an awkward silence. I stood up and left.

I went home and told Terry it didn't go very well, but in my own defense, the material didn't seem that funny. Before I could finish that sentence, I got a call from my agent, who told me to go to NBC in Burbank, where they wanted me to read the exact same pages for Brandon Tartikoff, the president of NBC, who was generally regarded as the emperor of television.

I drove to his office, where Bruce and all the producers were now gathered. After I read, Brandon asked me to wait outside. Minutes later, they all walked out of the office. Thomas Carter, the director, told me he would see me on Monday.

I went home thinking I would have to read this nonsensical medical terminology one more time on Monday. When I arrived home, I was greeted with a congratulatory phone call from my agent, who told me I got the job. I asked, "What is the job?"

He told me it was *St. Elsewhere*. It turns out that *St. Elsewhere* wasn't a sitcom. The show was a one-hour ensemble medical drama, which ended up airing for six years on NBC to great critical acclaim. I worked alongside the likes of William Daniels, who had played Dustin Hoffman's father in

The Graduate, Norman Lloyd, who was the star of Alfred Hitchcock's *Spellbound,* and a young actor named Denzel Washington. Our guest stars included Helen Hunt, Tim Robbins, and Kathy Bates.

Again, my life took a turn I had not expected. Four years earlier, I would have never guessed I would be doing stand-up comedy. Four days earlier, I would have never guessed I would be cast as a serious actor on a medical drama. Though my parents never said it, I was always concerned that they thought I was something of a loser. Now I could tell them that their son was becoming a doctor.

Speaking of medical dramas, I have to stop and tell you about the real-life medical drama that I am dealing with right now, which is making it very hard for me to concentrate on this book.

SEVEN

UH-OH

I don't know if this is an actual chapter or if it will survive the scissors of my editor, Philip Rappaport. And if it does, it's not for you, the reader. This chapter is for me. As cathartic as writing this book is, I'm right now in the midst of suffering a personal trauma. I have missed therapy for a while, so I would like to consider you, the reader, as my group. Let me just take you back a few months to give you some context.

It was January 2009, and I was in Toronto shooting *Howie Do It*, my hidden camera show that airs on NBC. I had a health scare. You may have read about it somewhere. There was a little thing going on with my heart. Until then, a health scare for me was accidentally touching the handrail on an escalator.

It started one day when I didn't even feel ill. That's unusual for me because I'm a hypochondriac, I'm obsessive-compulsive, and I'm always focused on something going wrong.

I was going through my production routine, meeting with the other producers and planning the pranks. Because I am the host of the show, I needed to have a physical for insurance purposes. Typically, this consists of a doctor coming to the office, asking a couple of questions, listening to your heart, and saying goodbye. On this particular day, the doctor showed up, asked me the questions, and, instead of saying goodbye, with the stethoscope still on my chest, said, "Uh-oh."

I'm not a doctor, but as you just read, I played one on TV. So I'm aware that when there is a stethoscope on your chest, "uh-oh" is not good.

"Why did you say 'Uh-oh'?" I asked.

"Are you aware of anything going on with your heart?" he asked.

"I know I'm inhaling and I'm exhaling, so I would imagine there is a lot going on with my heart," I said.

He sat back and folded his arms. "I'm being serious."

"I can't be serious, or I am going to scream and cry like a little girl. What do you hear?"

"I don't like the way your heartbeat sounds," he said. "I am going to recommend that you go to a cardiologist immediately."

Within fifteen minutes, I was in a cardiologist's office. He walked into the room, had me open my shirt, put his stethoscope to my chest, and lo and behold, he said, "Uh-oh." Two uh-oh's in one day was a little too much for me.

Apparently, my heart's rhythm was off. I was told the condition I had was atrial fibrillation, which is incredibly common. As much as he was telling me that to put me at ease, two uh-oh's in one day was mentally paralyzing.

"There are many things that can be done, but let's start with the least invasive," he said.

"I don't like the word *invasive*, but I'll play. What is the least invasive?"

"I'm going to cardiovert you."

I thought to myself, Fantastic. He's going to cardiovert me rather than doing something invasive. I asked him what this procedure entailed. Number one, he was going to give me drugs and anesthetize me. Why would I need drugs and anesthesia for a noninvasive procedure? They were then going to take a scope and jam it down my throat into my heart to make sure I didn't have existing clots that could cause a stroke during the actual cardioversion. If it's clear, they will make sure I am completely out cold, take a defibrillator—those two electric paddles you see in movies—press them against my chest, scream, "Clear!" and electrocute my heart back into normal rhythm. If this was considered noninvasive, I didn't even want to ask what the invasive procedure was.

The cardiologist explained to me that this was an easy procedure. I explained to him, "No, flossing is an easy procedure, and you don't have to yell, 'Clear!'"

I left the—I don't even know where it was I left, I'm drawing a blank—but I left wherever I was in a haze, numb with fear. I thought that the best thing to do was to call Terry and other family members, not to tell them that I was having this procedure, but to say how much I loved them. They had no idea that I was actually calling to say goodbye. I made small talk to check that nobody was angry at anything. I told them all that I would talk to them tomorrow, but I didn't believe I would hear their voices ever again.

The next day was a gloomy and overcast Wednesday in Toronto. I checked myself into the hospital. I lay down on the gurney, and they put an IV drip in my arm.

The next thing I remember was waking up and the doctor saying: "It's done. You're back in rhythm." He told me to come back Monday for a follow-up.

I got up off the gurney to put on my clothes. I discovered that they had shaved random patches of my chest. I also saw what I believed to be burn marks from the defibrillator. They may have been only red marks, but ever since the sand flies were burned out of me, in my mind when I see a red mark, I've been horribly burned.

I thought I was fine, so I got on a plane Thursday and flew to New York. On Friday, I went on *Live with Regis and Kelly* and the *Today* show to promote *Howie Do It*. I flew back to Toronto on Saturday, and then Monday I returned to the cardiologist for the follow-up.

The cardiologist listened to my chest and guess what he said? "Uh-oh, it's back." Hearing "uh-oh" from the cardiologist the second time was worse than hearing it the first time.

He then informed me that he was going to cardiovert me again at five p.m. the following day. I pointed out that it hadn't worked the first time and asked what else he could do. He said, "I don't want to tell you what the further options are." When somebody says he doesn't want to tell you, I get concerned.

There was no reason for me to be concerned, but I was. Then he added, "We're not there yet."

"You have no idea where I am," I said. "I'm making funeral arrangements. I now have to call more people and say goodbye. I'm running up a huge phone bill. I only have so many minutes on my plan."

I knew that I was going to be put under again. Anybody who has had any surgery or procedure knows that you can't eat or drink before you're given anesthesia. I skipped breakfast and went right to work. This was the one place where I could distract myself from my health issues. I didn't eat lunch, either.

We wrapped around four-thirty in the afternoon, and I had a driver take me to the hospital. Everybody else went back to the hotel to have a couple of drinks and eat dinner. They had plans. I was checking into the emergency room.

The procedure was repeated. Back on the gurney, IV drip, and two electronic plates pressed to my chest—and "Clear!"

When I woke up, the doctor told me that he tried twice but could not get my heart back in rhythm. My resting heart rate at that particular time was 160 beats per minute. Even though I was lying there, my heart rate was equivalent to what it would have been had I been running a marathon. So he gave me medication to lower my heart rate.

I was still a little groggy from the anesthesia, but I remember him telling me that I had to come back in a couple of days for another follow-up. I got off the gurney, checked out, and got a ride back to the hotel.

During the ride back, I called my road manager, Rich

Thurber, and told him that I needed to eat. I hadn't had any food or liquid since yesterday. I walked into the lobby of this bustling Sheraton Hotel where we were staying. Rich and several of the cast and crew were waiting for me, along with my mother.

I told them I wanted to go up to my room first to put on a sweater. It was January in Toronto, so I was cold. I think I needed an extra layer because they had shaved off my natural layering. I had never realized how warm little swatches of chest hair keep you in the winter.

I walked across the busy lobby to get on the elevator. I never press a public button with the end of my finger. So as I moved my knuckle to touch the Up button, it seemed to move away from me. I thought that was a little weird. Then I looked at the wall and it was also moving.

The next thing I remember was waking up on the floor, looking at the Sheraton lobby ceiling, lying in a puddle of my own urine. I don't know how long I was out. There was a huge crowd watching paramedics work on me. The buttons on my shirt were undone, and they were tapping on my erratically shaved chest. I was aware that I had pissed myself but didn't have the energy to get up and find a puddle or a ditch to fall in.

I was sure that I had just had a massive heart attack. I wasn't even sure I was still alive. I thought maybe I was on the other side, which I must say looked very similar to this side. There were a lot of people I knew and paramedics. If you believe in life after death, why can't there be paramedics there?

People were yelling my name very loudly over and over:

"Howie! Howie! Howie!" I was saying, "What? What?" But I was thinking, Can't you see I was just unconscious? Give me a moment.

The paramedic kept saying, "If you can hear me, squeeze my hand."

I didn't want to shake hands even in this condition, so I said, "No!"

"Why?" he asked in a concerned voice.

"I don't do that," I muttered as I tried unsuccessfully to lift my hand and give him a fist bump.

The paramedics loaded me on a gurney and took me to St. Michael's Hospital.

I ended up in the emergency room, which played on so many different fears of mine. I thought I was on my deathbed. As precarious as I believed my physical status was, all my focus was on my mental issues. I was lying on a filthy gurney soaked with my own urine in a small room along with many other sick people. This was my worst nightmare.

After they drew every conceivable fluid from me, taped a mess of wires to my chest, and gave me an echocardiogram, it became clear that I had not had a heart attack. I had passed out because I hadn't eaten, I was dehydrated, and I was full of chemicals from my procedure.

I felt weak, so I asked for something to eat. The nurses had ordered pizza and offered me a slice. Not only did it look delicious, it was a great distraction from my demons. The smell of melted cheese wafted into my nose as I picked up a slice. I was about to bring it to my mouth.

Now, you have to remember I was in the emergency room

on a gurney. I was separated by whoever else was in that room by nothing but a curtain.

At the moment the pizza hit my lips, I heard projectile vomiting from the next gurney, followed by gagging and alarm bells. Needless to say, I couldn't eat. I put down the pizza and screamed, "Get me out of here!" I'm sure my heart rate surpassed 160 at that point.

The nurses responded by rushing me upstairs to a semiprivate room on the cardiac floor. Semiprivate meant I had a roommate. He was an elderly Italian gentleman who had just undergone quadruple bypass surgery.

I had refused to get undressed, so I was lying in bed fully clothed. My roommate was wearing a standard-issue hospital gown. He would get out of bed and walk over to the window to look at the moon. While he was looking at the moon, I was left to stare at his moon. It was very disconcerting.

At this point, news of my hospitalization had hit TMZ before I had a chance to call my family. My daughter called me crying, asking if I was okay. I assured her I was.

As luck would have it, the medication lowered my heart rate. I was told I would be fine if I just kept taking the medication. The doctor asked me to return a week later to make sure the dosage was correct and my heart was still in rhythm.

I went back a week later, and of course, my rhythm was off. It was explained to me that I didn't have a plumbing problem, I had an electrical problem. Our heart is beating because there is an electrical signal shocking it—"tdzut, beat, tdzut, beat. . . ." But mine goes "tdzut tdzut, beat. . . ." I hope I spelled that right.

• • •

At the end of March, I flew back to Los Angeles. Even though I had been taking my meds continually, the symptoms were becoming progressively worse. I had become weaker, short of breath, and dizzy.

As soon as I met with my new cardiologist, Dr. Cannom, he recommended a procedure called an ablation. I immediately assumed this was the invasive procedure I had not been told about when I was first diagnosed in January as a broken-hearted comedian. I sat there silently for a minute, contemplating whether I should ask him to explain this procedure. I concluded I had no choice.

Dr. Cannom explained the procedure more eloquently, but this is how it sounded to a fearful, neurotic layman: They would rip a gaping hole in your groin, through which they jammed a camera and a laser gun. These instruments would tear their way past your stomach, spleen, and intestines on the way up into the interior chambers of your heart. Once there, they would search for the area where the electrical charge was misfiring. Once found, the area would be shot with a laser and burned beyond recognition.

Along with the many issues I had with this procedure, the first question I had was "Why do they have to enter through the groin?" I personally didn't care about the scar. I told the doctor that I thought the neck or shoulders would be a lot closer and easier. But he explained the only route was through the groin. I found it fascinating that whether it is a romantic encounter or a medical procedure, the way to a man's heart is always through his groin.

Before he had finished his explanation, I had already decided this was not for me.

"I don't want to do that," I told him.

"I think that's eventually going to be the answer, but I can first try another medication," he said.

He explained that he would need to keep a close eye on my condition. I was fitted with a monitor that I had to wear 24/7.

I am wearing one as I write this. The monitor consists of several wires attached to nodes that are stuck to my chest. The wires feed into a transmitter that is synced with a BlackBerry clipped to my pants. The device is monitored by LifeWatch, based in Chicago.

Here's how it works. When my heart goes out of rhythm, the BlackBerry automatically calls LifeWatch, and they, in turn, call me and ask, "How are you feeling?" I tell them, "You know how I'm feeling, otherwise you wouldn't be calling. Sorry I can't talk now, I can't breathe."

To distract myself from my heart problems, I went online and looked up notables who passed away in 2009. I learned that Marilyn Chambers and Ricardo Montalbán had died. As I scrolled down the list and studied the causes of death, my wife came into the room and saw what I was doing. She told me to stop looking at the death list and find something else.

So I went on Amazon.com to check what number this book is. I did this in April, seven months before the book was even published and only six and a half chapters into the writing process. It was number 1,566,167, which fascinated me, because it was not yet written, let alone on sale. I'm not sure I'll make it that far. But once the book is written and actually available, I'm hoping it will move up the list.

On May 1, 2009, I'm lying in bed watching TV at the MGM Grand in Las Vegas. The breaking news is that Danny Ganz, a venerable Las Vegas performer, has just died of heart failure at fifty-two. So I quickly turn off the TV.

For the next couple of days, my life becomes incredibly hellish. I'm terribly weak. I can't breathe. Every time I'm out in public, people are saying to me, "Can you believe that Danny Ganz died of a heart attack? He was only fifty-two." They have no idea that they are talking to a fifty-three-year-old who has wires taped to his chest attached to a BlackBerry. Coinciding with this moment, some strangers from Chicago are seeing a readout of an erratic heart beating at a rate of 160.

I spend each and every day conserving my energy so that I can get up onstage and be funny for an hour and a half. Every moment onstage, I'm trying not to fall down and die—and I don't mean dying as a comedian does with bad material, I mean dying as in Danny Ganz, Marilyn Chambers, and Ricardo Montalbán.

I have to say, writing this chapter is giving me more palpitations. The bell on my heart monitor is ringing. LifeWatch is now calling. I have to go. I hope I survive and I'm able to talk to you in the next chapter.

EIGHT

HOWIE LOU'S A FRIEND

My entire life is about distracting myself from horrible thoughts that constantly creep into my head. If I'm not doing something productive, I will find something to distract me. These distractions come upon me impulsively. Many people seek relief from their demons through food, alcohol, or drugs. My drug of choice is humor, sometimes at others' expense. I can't tell you how many times I end up regretting what I have done. In those instances, I would have been better off living with my demons. Here are two examples I can promise you I'm not proud of.

I had begun *St. Elsewhere,* and my notoriety was soaring. I had also become much more comfortable in Los Angeles because a small group of friends from Toronto had moved out.

My two closest friends were Michael Rotenberg, who would become my lawyer and later my manager, and my first comedy friend, Lou Dinos, who became my opening act.

St. Elsewhere was going on summer hiatus, and I was about to embark on a sixty-city tour sponsored by a beer company. Lou could not have been more excited. He would call me every day and give me the countdown: "Ten more days to go! Nine more days to go!" He was driving me crazy. One day for no other reason than a fun distraction, I decided to burst his bubble, though I didn't premeditate where I was going with the prank.

As he did every day, Lou called and announced, "Six more days to go!"

I stopped him. "Lou, Lou, hang on," I said. "I don't know how to tell you this. I have some bad news . . . you're not going on tour."

"How can that be?" he said. "It's six days away, and we are going for three months. . . ."

"It's ridiculous, but I'm fighting it."

"Tell me what happened."

"I will tell you exactly what happened," I improvised. "The beer company is funding the tour. For me to fly my opening act to every city will cost too much money. Your airfare alone is well over twenty thousand dollars. What they want to do is have a radio station in each market hold a contest to pick a local opening act." I knew he couldn't afford to pay his way.

"Oh, my God . . . ," he said, his voice trailing off. "What am I going to do? It's not like I can book clubs now. I was counting on this for rent money. I'm going to lose my apartment. What can I do?"

"Please, Lou, leave it with me," I reassured him. "I'm going to see if I can pull some strings."

I hung up the phone, leaving Lou destroyed. Terry was standing next to me. She told me that was incredibly mean and that I should call him back. She was right, but for reasons I can't explain there was no turning back for me. Instead, I called Michael Rotenberg, who was my lawyer at the time. I told him what I had done to Lou, and I asked him to play along with this concept. Then I called Mark Tinker, one of the producers of *St. Elsewhere,* and told him to also play along.

Mark knew Lou from another practical joke I had played on Lou. In that one, I told Lou that I had landed him a guest spot on an episode of *St. Elsewhere.* I had explained that there were no costumes, so he should wear his own clothes. He was playing an accident victim, so we doused him in fake blood. For two days, we had him sit in every scene soaked in blood . . . just out-

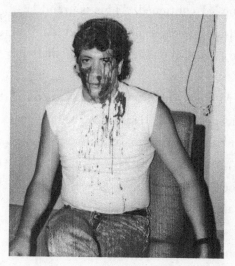

side the frame of the camera. Of course, Lou didn't know this.

At one point, we were filming a scene in a boardroom with all the other actors. Lou was sitting at the end of the table, covered in blood. He said, "Can I ask a question? Why would I be in a boardroom?" I told him that his condition was so critical that we wanted to keep an eye on him. Until he sat at home and watched the episode, he had no idea he wasn't in it.

As mean as that prank was, it paled in comparison with telling Lou he was no longer taking part in my summer tour.

I called Lou back. "I'm devastated," he said. "What's going to happen? How can we do this?"

"Lou, I'm going to loan you money for your rent because they came up with one solution that's so ridiculous that I cannot have a friend do this," I said.

"I'll do it!" he said. "Just tell me what it is."

"Okay, but I'm telling you I do not want you to do this, and I will pay your rent." I told Lou that Michael Rotenberg had negotiated a deal with the airline for a special spouse fare. "If you travel as the spouse of somebody, you go free."

"Okay . . . ," he said, growing excited.

"But here's the thing," I continued. "This is grand larceny, because we are defrauding the airline. If we act like you are the spouse, it's like twenty thousand dollars of theft in ticket revenue."

He cut me off. "I'm willing to do it. What do I have to do?"

"Here's what Michael negotiated," I said. "We will pay for all of your clothes, your hair, and your makeup. But you have to travel as a woman to qualify for the fare."

"Are you serious?" he asked.

"Dead serious," I said. "But if you don't want to do it, I will loan you the rent money."

"No, I gotta do it," he said.

"It's got to be totally your decision, because I think it's crazy, and I wouldn't do it," I said.

"I have no choice," he said.

I did, but I chose to keep going.

So we sent him over to the *St. Elsewhere* wardrobe department. Playing it completely straight on Mark's orders, they gave him a dress and a wig shorter than his own hair. They put a little bit of makeup on his cheeks. His hairy legs were exposed, and he had a five o'clock shadow. There was no reason whatsoever for anyone to even remotely mistake this creature for a woman.

He packed his normal clothes and sent them in a trunk on a separate flight with all my clothes and equipment, as we always did. We were flying from Los Angeles to Philadelphia and then taking a limo to Atlantic City for the first stop on the tour.

When it came time to leave for the airport, Terry pulled me aside and told me that I had to take a pair of his pants with me. I told her it was funnier to just let it play out. She promptly stopped speaking to me.

Lou and I headed for the airport in a limousine. It's the only time where the driver never talked to me. He was driving Howie Mandel and the worst possible cross-dresser. Thank God TMZ didn't exist yet.

We arrived at the terminal. Lou was wearing a dress and his baseball jacket, smoking a cigarette, and looking completely miserable. I don't think he realized what he had gotten himself into or how he would feel out in public dressed like this. It wasn't under the guise of being funny, but rather out of the desperation of not losing his apartment.

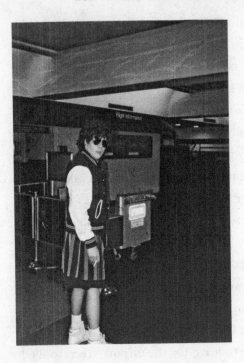

At check-in, a couple with their kids recognized me from *St. Elsewhere* and asked for an autograph. Being the comedian that he is, Lou walked over to me and put his arm around me very effeminately. In the middle of the autograph, the mother grabbed the kids' hands and pulled them away, as if to say, "This is not a good place for our children to be. Howie Mandel is a freak."

I turned around to Lou, grabbed him by his coat as hard as I could, and threw him up against the wall. "What the fuck do you think you are doing!" I said to him.

"If I'm going to be dressed like this, I want to have some fun with it," he said.

"You can have fun on your own time," I lectured him. "This is grand larceny. This is twenty thousand dollars of theft under my name. We could both end up in prison!"

Lou started to tremble. "Howie, I'm so sorry," he said. His voice was quivering. He sulked over to a chair and sat down. I snapped a picture.

I went to the ticket counter and switched his seat from first class to the last row of coach, next to my road manager, Jim, who was in on the gag. I told Jim not to answer any questions, just let Lou do all the talking. I had left the ticket in the name of Lou Dinopoulos, because I figured at some point he would have to make up some explanation that his real name was Louise.

I then boarded the plane and sat in my aisle seat in first class. The rest of the two hundred passengers began to board. As people passed me, I heard them saying, "Did you see that guy in the dress?" One little girl said, "Mommy, that was a man, wasn't it?" Everyone was murmuring, talking about the guy in the dress. Nobody was calling Lou a her.

I know what you're thinking. This is mean. As I retell it, I know it is mean. I'm embarrassed. But as I was doing it, I didn't think any of those thoughts. Even if my wife had said, as she did, "Stop, I'm not going to talk to you." These are just words. The impulse to do something funny or outrageous always overrode any focused reasoning or ramifications. But when I lost Lou as a friend, it was real. It had a tangible, painful ramification. I never thought that could possibly happen, because that's not a thought process that worked for me in any way. That's not an excuse; it's just the way it was.

Anyway, I didn't know what was going through Lou's mind, but for some reason he decided to board last, after everyone else was seated. When he finally walked onto the plane, there was complete silence. I've never heard an airplane loaded with two hundred passengers so quiet. He walked down the aisle, holding his coat in front of him. Because I had moved his seat to the rear of the plane, he had a long walk of shame. No one made eye contact. It was as if a ghost were boarding the plane.

I called over the flight attendants and told them the entire story. This was way before 9/11, and I was a comedian, so they played along. I said that he was scared to death of being caught. I told them that he thought he was traveling on an illegal spouse fare and that they should ask him as many questions as possible and act suspicious of his answers.

After the flight took off, the first flight attendant walked back to Lou's seat and asked for his and Jim's tickets. They handed her their tickets, and she walked back to the front of the plane. She told me that Lou's hand was shaking.

The flight attendant went back to Lou's seat and began to grill him. "I understand that you two are traveling on the spouse fare, but your names are different," she said. "The gentleman's ticket has a different name from the lady's, which says Dinopoulos. Why is that?"

Lou is desperately looking at Jim to answer, but Jim is staring out the window, ignoring him.

"I asked you a question," she repeated to Lou. "How come there are two different names when you are traveling on a spouse fare?"

Lou dug down deep, and in the worst falsetto imaginable, he looked up at her and said, "I kept my maiden name." It was not even a female voice; it was just a really bad impression of Mickey Mouse.

Hearing the horrible imitation of a woman, the flight attendant put her hand to her ear and pretended not to hear. "Pardon me?" she said.

Again, in his Mickey Mouse falsetto, Lou said, "I kept my maiden name."

She nearly lost it in a fit of laughter. She handed him his ticket and quickly turned away and walked toward the front of the plane. She told me that I had to hear his voice. Soon, the other flight attendants got in on the act. It became a game of going back and talking to the man dressed like a woman who sounded like Mickey Mouse. They would ask him if he wanted peanuts, another soda, or a blanket.

I told one of the flight attendants to tell him the captain would like to speak to him about his ticket. She did.

A few minutes later, Lou got out of his seat and began walking up the aisle. It was like a scene from *Dead Woman Walking.* He slowly made his way to the front. The people who had heard him were no doubt thinking that there was a crazy-ass gender bender among them and they didn't know what was going to happen next.

Lou reached my seat and stopped. The lady next to me stared purposefully at the movie. Lou looked down at me.

This was horrible, and I feel horrible retelling it.

I looked up at Lou. Out of the corner of his eye, a tear welled up and ran down his cheek. In his Mickey Mouse falsetto voice, he said, "I'm busted." He was clinging to the voice like a lifeline.

"What?" I asked, wanting to hear the voice again.

"I'm busted," he said, the falsetto cracking. "They got me."

I shook my head. "No, you're not," I said. "It's a joke."

Still in falsetto, he said, "What?"

"It's a joke," I repeated.

"What do you mean, it's a joke?" he falsettoed.

The lady beside me, for no reason, began to lean tightly against the window. She couldn't get far enough away from me or the freak I was talking to.

"It's been a joke from the beginning," I copped. "Michael knew it was a joke. Tinker and everyone else at *St. Elsewhere* knew it was a joke. There is no such thing as a spouse fare. It's just a funny joke."

I've never seen despair turn into anger faster. It was as if I had lit the fuse of a time bomb. He grabbed his wig, which was shorter than his hair, threw it as hard as he could at the movie screen, and yelled what sounded like the f-word but was so distorted that I can't say for sure. He grabbed the glass of orange juice off the tray of the lady beside me, threw it on me, and called me a very loud and I'm sure nasty name that, again, I couldn't make out. He ran into the bathroom and slammed the door.

Even though this was before 9/11, people were starting to look worried. Some guy in a dress had just lost it and was throwing drinks and slamming the bathroom door. Because the flight attendants were part of the joke, one of them made an announcement apologizing for the disruption. She explained that Howie Mandel the comedian was on board and was playing a joke on a friend on the way to his show in Atlantic City. Everybody settled down, probably relieved that a real lunatic cross-dresser wasn't on the plane.

Lou stayed in the bathroom for a half hour, scrubbing all the makeup off his face. Then he rushed by me and sat in his seat. After a few minutes, I looked back through the curtain and I could see his eyes above the seat line—pure anger. He gestured for me to come back. I walked back.

"Where are my pants?" he said with no trace of the falsetto.

"They're on the other flight with the equipment," I told him.

"I get the joke and I see where it was funny. Where are my fucking pants?"

"Your clothes are on a totally different flight."

"So I have to sit here for five hours in this dress?"

"Yeah, I'm sorry," I said, adding, "Maybe this went too far."

Finally we landed in Philadelphia. He knew where the car was picking us up. To get there as soon as possible, he sprinted through the airport, carrying his briefcase and his coat and smoking a cigarette. As I walked in his wake, I heard people saying, "Did you see that guy run through the airport wearing the dress?"

It was an hour-and-a-half drive to Atlantic City, and Lou didn't say a word the entire way, he just seethed. We arrived at the Sands Hotel and headed for the VIP check-in area. There was a line, so we waited. The check-in area was in the lobby attached to the casino, so people were beginning to notice the man in the dress. Lou was pacing, and a firestorm was brewing.

Then came the straw that broke the camel's back. A bus pulled up and a group of seventy-five middle-aged ladies from central Jersey got out, laughing and kibitzing among themselves. Most of them were wearing dresses that looked very similar to Lou's. The cackling bunch descended in a group on the casino, and soon Lou was stuck in the middle of the gaggle of ladies all wearing dresses similar to his.

Lou snapped. He broke through the crowd, past the waiting VIPs, to the front of the check-in line and confronted this poor young girl working at the desk. In the loudest, most primally desperate voice I've ever heard, he raged, "Give me my fucking room now!"

He was so loud that the place fell silent. The action in the casino just off the lobby came to a halt. The dice stopped. Cards went down. Everybody looked up from their gambling.

This small voice from behind the desk asked, "What's your name?"

"I'm with Howie Mandel, give me my key right now," he ordered.

It was like a bank robbery. She handed him a key, and he walked over to the elevator.

During this entire time, the place was in a state of suspended animation—all these women wearing dresses like his, the gamblers, the VIPs. He pressed the button. You could hear the ding. The door opened. He got in. The door closed, and then we resumed life as we knew it.

A few minutes later, I reached the VIP counter. I explained to the girl at the desk that we were playing a joke and that Lou's outburst was my fault. She looked down at her paperwork and informed me that she had given Lou the wrong room. Not knowing what would happen next, I told her to call him.

When she reached him and explained that she was nervous and had given him the wrong room, Lou let loose. The girl held the phone away from her ear, and I could hear him screaming at her. I could hear horrible obscenities coming from the other end of the phone.

I don't know this for a fact, but I think he was so distraught that he went up to his room, slammed the door, ripped off the dress, and threw it in the trash. In his rage, he picked up a lamp, smashed it, and then turned over the desk. So he was sitting there naked, a destroyed man in a destroyed room, being told that he needed to move.

She hung up the phone. "I don't think he wants to move," she said meekly.

"That's fine," I said. "I think I've gone too far."

In fact, I had. Lou didn't speak to me for a few days. He came to work, did his act, and went back to his room. I called my wife and apologized to her, though I didn't fill her in on all the details of the plane ride. I also apologized profusely to Lou. You would think I'd learned my lesson, but it didn't stop there.

I never could resist my impulses. I managed to almost get him evicted from his apartment. It happened when a friend of mine—Mark Blutman, a comic from Canada—had a nephew on a summer teen tour. The tour was visiting Los Angeles, so he checked the kid out for a day. Here's what we did.

We dirtied this little boy's clothes and gave him a battered suitcase and a note that I had written. I called Lou at around two a.m. Lou lived alone, so I knew he would be able to chat. I didn't know until later that he was lying in bed in his underwear. In the background, I heard the doorbell.

Lou expressed dismay over someone ringing his doorbell in the middle of the night. He put down the phone and looked through the peephole to see who it was. He came back and told me that there was a kid at the door.

"Bullshit, there's no kid there," I said.

"Yeah, there is," he said.

"Open the door and see what he wants," I encouraged.

Lou went back to the door and opened it. Standing in front of him was this disheveled kid clutching a suitcase. He handed Lou the note that I had written.

Lou and I had played clubs for years, so at this point I knew most of what had gone on. The note read: "Dear Lou. By the time you read this note I will no longer exist as you know me. A few years ago you played a club. You may not remember me, but I was a waitress there. We had what I believe was a great time that night. I never wanted to burden you with the responsibility. Standing in front of you is the seed of that night's experience. Two years ago I was diagnosed with cancer. I thought it was in remission, but apparently it wasn't. I never wanted to do this to you, but if you are reading this note, I have passed. Please take care of our son. Love, Wendy."

I know this makes me sound terrible, but this was what I wrote and gave to the kid to give to Lou.

Lou came back to the phone. I could hear the torture in his voice. "Howie," he said, his voice cracking, "you're not going to believe who's here."

"Who?" I asked.

He was on the verge of tears. "My son."

"What?"

"My son . . ." His voice trailed off, and then he mumbled something very spiritual and philosophical about how your life can change in one moment. "I have a son."

"You're lying to me," I said with mock incredulity. "Put the kid on the phone."

He put the kid on the phone. I told the kid to go sit on the bed, count to fifteen, scream as loud as he could, "Nobody loves me, nobody cares about me!" and then run as fast as he could out the door and down to the blue car, where his uncle was waiting for him. He said okay.

Lou came back on the phone. "I don't know what to do," he said. "This is such a huge responsibility."

In the background, I heard the kid scream, "Nobody loves me, nobody cares about me!" The next thing I heard was the receiver drop. And then I heard Lou's voice wailing, "I love you! I love you! I just want to care for you!"

This is at two in the morning. Lou lived on the second floor of an apartment building where all the units were connected by a breezeway. His neighbors were watching him running past their windows in his underpants, chasing after and screaming to a little boy that he loved him and wanted to care for him—not a very wholesome image.

The next day, I had to explain to his landlord that it had been a practical joke, because the man was ready to call the police and evict Lou from his apartment. Lou called his girlfriend, who later became his wife. She thought that it was so cruel that he should not be my friend anymore.

Do you, the reader, think less of me now? I admit there's no excuse for that kind of behavior, and I was 100 percent wrong for doing it. Now, this is not an excuse, but people have said to me, "It was so weird and far-fetched that he had to know something was fishy." The thing is that there is nobody more trusting than Lou Dinos, and the fact that he never suspected anything was wrong was too big a draw for me.

Lou is the most loyal friend anyone could ever have. I really made a big mistake because I ended up losing him as a close friend. Today, we talk to each other every so often, but he's not as close as he was. I did go too far and I'm the loser here. I learned my lesson.

I felt devastated afterward that I had made him that upset. Lou never had any sense of jealousy or competition, which makes what I did even more horrible. In fact, he called me the day after I wrote this chapter to tell me about his promotion at the insurance company where he now makes his living. I told him I was writing a book and including some of the old stories. Without missing a beat, he said, "You should tell the one about the time I wore the dress on the plane. That was really funny."

The seed of all comedy comes from dark, negative places. It's amazing that the day I was writing this story in the book, Lou called me and remembered. But the day that those things happened, I promise, was torture for him. Ultimately, however, as Lou points out, it is funny. If you can find the humor in these pranks, you have a sense of humor, which Lou clearly does. I don't condone this kind of behavior. I recognize the wrong and the funny at the same time, which is part of the dichotomy that is my life.

NINE

ANOTHER DAY AT THE ORIFICE

I t was now the mid-1980s, and I was incredibly content both personally and professionally. I was a regular on a network TV series, I was also touring the country doing stand-up, and my wife was pregnant with our first child. What else was there?

Warner Brothers called me—when I say Warner Brothers, I don't mean the actual brothers Jack and Sam, I mean executives in the company's music division—and offered me the opportunity to do an album. I was now to add recording artist to my repertoire. The concept was that they were going to send a crew to my various stand-up dates, record and edit them together, and voilà, I would have my first album. The tour was called the North American Watusi Tour. I know, it makes no sense, but that was the point.

I decided that this wasn't quite enough. I felt that if I was to be considered a legitimate recording artist, I had to have music on my album. A musician friend, Greg Chapman, and I wrote a silly little song entitled "I Do the Watusi." Warner Brothers loved the idea and funded a recording studio and a music video.

As far as comedy was from the path where I believed I would go in life, now I was sitting in a Hollywood recording studio with musicians playing my ridiculous song. To make this even more surreal, Warner Brothers hired Jellybean Benítez to help me produce this track. (Apparently, that's what they call it in music terminology.) I had no idea why they were so excited to have Jellybean working with me until I found out that he produced for Michael Jackson, Whitney Houston, and Madonna.

As excited as I was, I can only imagine the excitement Jellybean must have felt in being able to extend his list to include Michael Jackson, Whitney Houston, Madonna, and Howie Mandel—all of us music icons of the 1980s. I was also given some money to shoot a video, which premiered on MTV in 1984. It was not one of my proudest moments, but in my mind I was now a legitimate recording artist.

How many other monikers could I possibly add to this illustrious career? One more was to be added. I received a call from the Comedy Store. They'd had an inquiry as to the possibility of my performing fifteen minutes of stand-up at a house party for a huge fee. I thought, Wait a minute. I'm doing television, concerts, and cable specials, and now becoming a recording artist. My response was "No, I will not play at someone's house, but thank him for asking."

Shortly afterward, the phone rang again. It was the guy from the Comedy Store. "Is there any amount of money that you would take to do fifteen minutes at this house party?" he asked.

Without any thought and again on impulse, I blurted out, "Twenty-five thousand dollars," and hung up.

Minutes passed, and the guy was back on the line. "It's all set," he said. "You're on for fifteen minutes on Saturday night at his house in Benedict Canyon."

I began to worry. I was going to be paid twenty-five grand for fifteen minutes at somebody's house. This sounded like a scam. "I have to have the cash before I show up," I informed him, and once again hung up.

The guy called back. "You can pick up the cash in an hour," he said.

I got in my car and drove to the Comedy Store. Waiting for me was a giant wad of cash. This was too easy. I didn't have to pack a bag or get on a plane. All I had to do was drive my car to some guy's house and spend fifteen minutes entertaining him. For this I would be paid $25,000. There had to be more to it.

I asked my wife to join me. She declined, which turned out to be a wise decision on her part.

On Saturday night, I drove up Benedict Canyon, a long, winding, dark road in the Hills of Beverly. The more I thought about this gig, the more concerned I became. I was having flashes of the Manson family luring me into a trap. I began to get scared. I had no idea what I was heading into.

Near the top of Benedict, a young woman appeared out of

the darkness and flagged me down. She looked into my window. "You're Howie Mandel," she said. "Leave your car right here. This is the party."

I pulled over and parked. I didn't seem to be in front of any particular address. She walked me through a giant wall of hedges onto the grounds of an estate. I could hear what sounded like a party going on inside. She took me around the back past the pool into a small, dark space. She told me to wait in this room until I was introduced, because I was a surprise.

As she closed the door, I realized I was in a powder room, sandwiched between a toilet and a pedestal sink. There was one door leading outside and one apparently leading into the house. There was barely enough room to vote, let alone take care of business. I could hear the party on the other side of the door.

At this point in my career, my stand-up involved a large array of props, such as a handbag in the shape of a hand, lots of hats, and a plastic nose. I couldn't bring myself to put any of these down on a bathroom floor. I jostled the props to get them in some kind of order so I would be ready to take the stage.

In the middle of my preparation, the door from the house opened and a very intoxicated male partygoer entered. He didn't even flinch at the sight of a guy wearing a crazy hat and a fake nose standing by the toilet. He closed the door behind him, lowered his fly, and began to urinate. His shoulder was touching my back. My face was pressed against the wall. He didn't say anything. I couldn't breathe. My heart was palpitating. I was now thinking this gig wasn't worth $50,000. A strange man was pissing within inches of me. He finished and walked out—without washing his hands, I might add.

My OCD had been triggered. I was panic-stricken. I unspooled twenty-five feet of toilet paper, which I wrapped around my hand. This would be the tool I would use to pull the latch on the door and make my escape.

I waited in there for what seemed a long time. I can't tell you exactly how long. Finally I heard it.

"Ladies and gentlemen, Howie Mandel." I banged my protected hand on the latch, the door swung open, and with a wad of toilet paper and a dozen props in hand and on head I was onstage.

What I saw was the most surreal vision I have had to date. First of all, I just want to say that this room was spectacular. It looked like one of those palatial rooms from *Architectural Digest*. From the looks of the décor, I had grossly underpriced myself at $25,000 for fifteen minutes.

Here was the scene. There were maybe five guys, one of whom was the drunk guy who'd just pissed, and (as best as I could see) six women. For the most part, the women were not wearing anything. For that matter, neither were most of the guys. Some of the guys were in the midst of getting pleasured orally. Others were . . . well, let me just say that every possible orifice was in use. It looked like Fellini directing a film for Larry Flynt. Then, from the side of the room, a gentleman wearing no pants, leaning over in ecstasy with a woman attached to his member, said, "Please, oh, please, Howie, start your act."

My first thought was, Are you f—ing serious? But I had already taken the $25,000 and I didn't want any trouble, so I began. "Good evening, ladies and gentlemen. How is everyone tonight?"

I have to say, had this evening been recorded you might think I was doing well, but the screams and guttural cries of pleasure had nothing to do with my material. A few minutes into my act, a woman—who was under the couch with her ankles pulled up above her head, and with two men exploring her somewhat aggressively—had the presence of mind to ask me, "Could you do the Bobby voice?" Why not? I began to sing, "It's my potty and I'll cry if I want to." Over to my right, one of the gentlemen was pleasuring one of the females orally. I grabbed a small dish of guacamole and tapped him on the shoulder. As he looked up, I asked if he would like some dip with that. Before I knew it, my fifteen minutes were up and I was off into the night.

I came to realize—no pun intended—that the guy who'd asked me to begin happened to be the CEO of a hugely successful corporation that still exists today. It was his bachelor party.

A week later, I was walking through the Galleria, a mall in the San Fernando Valley. A lady came up to me and said that she loved my comedy. She added that her husband was at a bachelor party a week ago and he had told her that I was the entertainment. Before I could answer, I noticed a man twenty feet behind her signaling frantically at me.

Click. It dawned on me that this guy happened to be one of the partygoers. I realized that I had been hired as a decoy so all these guys could go home and honestly say to their wives,

"You're not going to believe it, but So-and-so hired Howie Mandel to do a private performance for us in his living room." Up until now, I had been a comedian, actor, and recording artist whose sole purpose was to entertain. But now I had also become a decoy whose mission it was to save marriages. I learned one more lesson that night . . . well, not so much a lesson as two more positions.

My new role of marriage decoy was important to me. I held the institution of marriage in very high esteem. As I didn't yet have children, my marriage was the most important thing in my life, and Terry was the most important person in my life. God bless her with what she has had to put up with, not only with my personal mental craziness but also with the craziness in the world of show business. Therein lies a story.

As much as I enjoy my notoriety, Terry, unlike me, has absolutely no desire for attention. She cherishes her anonymity so much that I had to convince her to be photographed for our wedding album. That being said, my recognition has really affected Terry's life. This was never more apparent than during the birth of our first child, Jackie.

The hours leading up to the actual birth were a potpourri of emotions—excitement, terror, exhaustion, and, most of all for Terry, humiliation. Jackie was to be born December 14, 1984, right in the middle of the *St. Elsewhere* run. Not unlike most other parents, we decided to give birth in a hospital. *St. Elsewhere* was a medical show that takes place in a hospital setting, so it obviously attracted a large following in medical circles. What *Sex and the City* later meant to women, *St. Elsewhere* meant to doctors.

Word spread quickly that Dr. Fiscus—the name of my character—was in the house. As much as I appreciated the fact that people in the medical community admired the show, and as much as I personally craved the attention, my poor wife once again was about to become the victim. There had been times when an anxious fan physically shoved her out of the way to share a moment with me. There had been times when women publicly propositioned me right in front of her, as if she didn't exist. She has faced her share of disrespect as a result of my notoriety. But this next transgression tops them all.

Terry was in the midst of labor, contracting every eleven minutes. This did not seem to deter the doctors who all paraded in to share some face time. These doctors were aware of the personal nature of the situation, so each decided to give his visit a veiled purpose to discount any possible discomfort.

The door would open. A doctor would say hello, introduce himself, and ask how things were going—all the while pulling on a latex glove. He would then insert a finger into my wife and tell me which episode or scene from the show was his favorite. Once the conversation was finished, he would remove the finger and inform us that my wife had dilated to four centimeters.

After about the fifth doctor, Terry put her foot down, which made it much harder for the doctors to insert their fingers into her vagina.

When it comes to dilating, I think one doctor is enough. You don't need a consensus, but apparently for those few hours, my wife's vagina took over the title of decoy for the actual purpose of this party.

Once again, I'm using this book to apologize to the love of my life, Terry. That particular story was not going to be in the book until Terry herself reminded me of it while laughing hysterically. In fact, she said, "I still have the fingerprints on my labia." Terry can find the humor in everything. This is the key to the success of our marriage. But I won't lie and tell you we don't have bumps in the road. Humor always seems to rescue us from the precipice.

There is one particular example when Terry told me: "That's it, I'm out!" She ran to the door, turned to me very dramatically, and declared, "**I will send for my things!**"

I waited a beat and then asked, "What did you just say?"

She repeated, "I will send for my things."

First of all, I had never heard that statement outside of a movie. So I asked, "Who will you send and what specific things will you be sending them for?"

After a long, dramatic, painstaking pause, a smile appeared on Terry's face. And then slowly she began to laugh. So did I. There are very few women who would find the humor in this otherwise serious situation. As we both laughed together at the absurdity of her statement, we embraced. The fight was over.

As I write this, we are still going strong after thirty-six years together. I cannot tell you how much I love and respect her and how lucky I am to have found this girl.

So all of her things remain to this day. No one was ever sent to take them away. And life went on.

TEN

THE LITMUS
TEST

Here's where I was. I was a father, a headlining comedian, one of the stars of a network television show, a recording artist, and a decoy, yet I felt there was still something missing, the one goal I set for myself. Regardless of all these accomplishments, the one badge of honor one needed to be considered a successful comedian was an appearance on *The Tonight Show*, commonly referred to as the Johnny Carson show.

I never really understood that thinking. When I told people I was a comedian, without hesitation they would inevitably ask, "Have you ever been on the Johnny Carson show?"—as if to say, without this credit, you're not a comedian. Well, what am I?

I remember being devastated the night that Jim McCawley, who was the show's chief booker, came to see me do a set at the Comedy Store. It didn't matter how well you did, it was all about delivering something they believed Johnny would like. Those doing the show were mostly monologists, like David Brenner and George Carlin, who would hold up mirrors to the minutiae of our lives. That's so not what I did. In fact, I was the opposite of what was being booked. I used rubber gloves, props, and funny sounds. After my set, Jim told me: "Not only am I not going to book you on *The Tonight Show*, you will never be on *The Tonight Show*."

Mike Douglas loved me. Merv Griffin loved me—I did *Merv* fourteen times. I had performed on HBO. But it looked as if I would be forever telling people that I hadn't done Carson.

At that time, Joan Rivers was Johnny's favorite guest host. Her ratings were through the roof. She was a superstar in comedy. I had heard that Joan was coming out to Los Angeles for a week to fill in for Johnny. I knew that she worked out her material at the Comedy Store.

So when I called for spots, I had them book one immediately before Joan's appearance. They always ran behind, so I figured that when she arrived for her set, she would inevitably see me.

As luck would have it, I woke up the morning of my showcase aching all over. It turned out I had a temperature of 103. I had the flu. I thought I was going to die. I will clarify that by saying I don't think there is a day when I don't think I am going to die. But this time I had a really high fever and I was nauseated. This was one of the few times when my mind and my body were in sync.

I don't know how, but I pulled myself together. I knew this was my only chance to ever be on *The Tonight Show*. I got in my little yellow Honda with the black racing stripes and headed for the Comedy Store. I was so dizzy as I made my way through the snakelike Laurel Canyon that I was sure I was going to crash.

I arrived a sweaty mess. I went backstage, guzzled water, and sat with my head in my hands. Just before I went on, Joan Rivers walked into the room. I thought, I have just made the biggest mistake of my life. I'm going to be seen by Joan Rivers. I've already been told by Jim McCawley that not only will I not be on *The Tonight Show* with Johnny, I will never be on. Now I feel that if Joan sees me in this condition, I'll never be on any show she does. So I'm about to create a wider swath of places I'm not welcome.

As I'm questioning myself, I hear the announcer say, "Our next guest is Howie Mandel." I know that Joan Rivers is in the room. I take the stage sweating and dizzy, and for the life of me, I can't tell you what I did. But what I said first got a big, hard laugh.

That always happens to me. When I go out on the road and don't feel well, whether I'm having heart palpitations or I'm just sick, as soon as I get that first laugh, it's like a warm blanket covering me. Nothing else exists in the world except for that laughter. My physical issues fall by the wayside, my mind goes blank, and I'm in another world.

That night, I was in that other world, and this warm blanket of laughter was splashing over me. It was one of the best sets I had done. I really enjoyed me. The audience enjoyed me, too. After seven minutes, I said good night, and the audience roared.

As I walked toward the back of the room, Joan Rivers passed me on her way to the stage and said, "Very funny."

That was it? That's all? What had I just accomplished? I rose from my sickbed to perform, but after the laughter died down, I felt sicker. It's like having the flu and opening the door to get some fresh winter air. It might be relieving for a minute, but you end up with pneumonia. I thought, I'll wait. Maybe she has more to say to me than "Very funny."

I walked down the stairs onto Sunset Boulevard and sat down. I could hear roars of laughter and excitement as Joan did her act. I was fading.

After I heard Joan say "Good night" to an even louder roar from the audience, I thought, Okay, she's going to leave and walk by me, and my career will be changed forever.

But she didn't come out. I guess she was staying and talking to other comedians and enjoying herself. Where did she have to run to? I had to go back to my sickbed, but she felt fine. So I waited and I waited and I waited. A half hour went by. Forty-five minutes. An hour. Maybe even two hours. I don't know, but it was an eternity.

The place was emptying out. It was very late at night. I was sitting like a crumpled little glob of death at the bottom of the stairs. Then I heard Joan's voice. She was talking to somebody and walking down the stairs toward me. I forced myself to stand up, leaning against the wall so I wouldn't fall over. When she reached me, I said, "You were so funny."

On the set of *Little Monsters*. Fred Savage and I with director Richard Greenberg. I spent the entire day in my rubber.

As the host of Expo 86 in Vancouver, I got to meet Prince Charles and Lady Diana. Thank God I was still shaking hands. I don't think the fist bump would've gone over.

Look at all the crap I dropped all over the stage at Carnegie Hall. Just like my cousin Itzhak Perlman. (He really is my cousin.)

My first appearance with Johnny. The litmus test was positive. I was now considered a comedian.

Radio City. What a night.

Right: On the set of *Walk Like a Man*.

Below: With my *Walk Like a Man* cast mates.

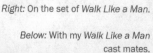

With one of my heroes, Richard Pryor, about a year before he died.

With my alter ego Bobby from *Bobby's World*.

The Howie Mandel Show: first show, first guest Jennifer Aniston. We were allowed to talk about anything but Brad Pitt.

I was also the voice of Gizmo in *Gremlins*. What a range—I used the exact same voice for Bobby.

Hair today.

Gone tomorrow.

My fam, 2002. Me, Riley, Alex, Terry, and Jackie.

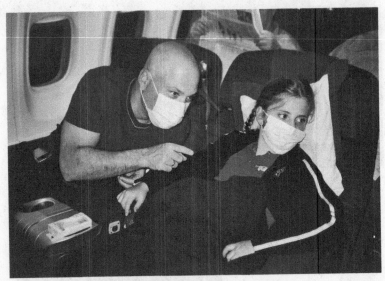

Just another day of travel with Dad, the germaphobe, for Riley Mandel.

Terry and I in the blue room of the White House having coffee with the Clintons, the Gores, and the Chrétiens—the prime minister of Canada and his wife. Who woulda thunk?

I'm now a puppet on *Sesame Street* who plays Meal or No Meal.

I ask you: deal or no deal?

Everybody was playing Deal, even Oprah on her show May 4, 2007.

I've arrived: a star on the Hollywood Walk of Fame, September 4, 2008.

"You were really funny," she replied.

I mustered all my strength. "Thank you so much. Coming from you that means a lot."

"Have you ever been on *The Tonight Show?*" she asked.

To which I responded, "No, but Wednesday is my birthday."

She smiled. "Have your agent call tomorrow."

I felt as if I had died and gone to heaven. This was the good kind of dying, not the dying I had been feeling up until that moment.

My agent called, and *The Tonight Show* booked me for the following week with Joan as the host. Though I was never going to be on the show with Johnny Carson, it was still *The Tonight Show*. It was worth coming so close to death and risking my life to perform in front of Joan Rivers.

Let me explain how an appearance on *The Tonight Show* worked. Comics would come onstage and perform. If they were good, they would be invited back. But the real key to success was being asked by Johnny to join him on the couch after your performance. Making it to the couch was the brass ring.

Luck happened to be on my side. Joan booked me as one of the stars of the hit NBC show *St. Elsewhere.* So rather than being introduced and doing my stand-up act, I would go directly to the couch. I approached it as I would doing stand-up. I put together the routine that I wanted to do. In a preinterview, I gave cues to Joan in the form of questions that would trigger these comedy pieces. By her asking me how I was, I could launch into my prostate exam routine directly from my stand-up act.

When I arrived at the NBC Studios in Burbank, I felt as though I had climbed a mountain and reached the pinnacle of my career. It was the scariest, most exciting feeling on earth. I thought that every eye in America would be on me at eleven-thirty that night. This was *The Tonight Show*, the *Ed Sullivan Show* of our time. I had heard stories about Elvis and the Beatles performing on *Ed Sullivan*. This was the night that Howie Mandel was going to be on *The Tonight Show*. In my mind, however I wore my hair that night, that's how everybody would be wearing it next week.

I went on, and my seated performance did as well as any of my stand-ups. Afterward, I felt that if nothing else happened in my career, I had made it. From that night forward, when I told people I was a comedian and they asked me if I had been on *The Tonight Show*, I could say, "Yes." I was a comedian.

But it got better. The next day, I received a call from *The Tonight Show*. Johnny had watched me and wanted me to come back when he was there. I could not believe this was happening. What a twist of fate. Just a few months earlier, I had been told I would never be on the show, but I had made it happen. Now I would be on twice in three weeks—and the second time with *the* Johnny Carson.

I had set my precedent. Even though it was with Johnny, I was still going to do my comedy from the couch. But there was a protocol. I had to go over everything I was going to do so there were no surprises. I called Jim McCawley and told him all the bits I had planned—except one. I knew he would not let me do it if I told him. I was sure it would either make me or break me on *The Tonight Show.* If it did break me, at least I was going down on the biggest forum in comedy.

The big night arrived. Standing backstage, just hearing Johnny Carson's voice saying, "Ladies and gentlemen, Howie Mandel," was like an out-of-body experience. I made my way to the couch and was mesmerized by the image of Johnny. He had been a staple in my house since childhood. Now here he was without the frame of a TV set around him. He asked me a question. I answered. Big laugh. He asked me a second of the planned questions. Bigger laugh. This continued throughout our preset routine. And now the moment of truth.

I had reached break point. I was ready to take the chance. I could hear what would become the Nike catchphrase screaming in my head: Just Do It!

I asked Johnny if he liked 3-D movies. He seemed to be taken aback, as if to say, "Where is this going?" Having no choice, he replied that he did. I pulled out a pair of those silly 3-D cardboard glasses and actually asked Johnny Carson, the king of late-night comedy, to put them on. He did.

Next, I pulled out a small stuffed animal. I could only imagine the horror on Jim McCawley's face as he was watching the monitor backstage. And then with reckless abandon, I threw it at Johnny's face. It hit him right between the eyes. "Doesn't it look like it's coming right at you?" I said.

His response seemed to take an eternity. Finally . . . he sat back in his seat and just started laughing. The audience joined him. I had arrived.

I went on to appear on twenty-one episodes with Johnny Carson. Then came the day I probably went too far.

I was in the middle of shooting a Blake Edwards movie entitled *A Fine Mess*. Jim McCawley called me on the set three hours before *The Tonight Show* taped and said that Sammy Davis Jr., the lead guest, had backed out for health reasons. Jim, who had now become a friend of mine, told me he was really in a jam and begged me to come on the show.

"I'll be honest with you," I told Jim. "I'm shooting a movie. I've got absolutely nothing."

I knew how they operated. They needed a set routine. The last time there had been a surprise was probably when I whipped the stuffed animal at Johnny. I myself was also pretty meticulous about my television appearances. I told Jim that I didn't have time to come up with seven minutes of good material, run it by him, and prepare to perform it all in the next three hours.

Finally, I relented. "Jim, I will do it, but here's the deal," I said. "I'll try to come up with something, but I won't have time to go over it with you. Are you okay with that?"

He said that he was. I hung up the phone and thought, Now what? I started wandering around the studio, searching for ideas. I ended up in the art department, where I spotted a thirty-foot-long saber-toothed tiger made of plaster. I asked one of the guys how much it would cost to put it on a dolly and ship it to NBC in Burbank.

I negotiated with the guy and settled on $500. I wasn't even sure why I was asking for the saber-toothed tiger. I seemed to be an audience to my own life.

For whatever reason, my attention was then drawn to the left-hand corner of the room, where there was a giant carrot.

I pointed to the carrot—and I heard myself say, as though I believed it was a great idea, "Is there any way you could tie the carrot on top of the saber-toothed tiger?" The guy looked at me strangely, nodded, and proceeded with the help of two other men to tie the carrot on top of the tiger. To this day, I have no idea why I wanted this.

I then called Jim McCawley and told him there was something coming and they needed to accept delivery. He didn't ask what it was, and I didn't tell him. He agreed and said, "This is going to be great, thank you so much, Howie."

A few hours later, I'm standing behind the curtain at *The Tonight Show*, ready to go on. The guy who opened the curtain had become my friend over my twenty-one previous appearances. He was always incredibly warm and friendly. This time he's just looking at me and at the giant saber-toothed tiger with a carrot tied on top as if I'm an idiot. I begin to feel nauseated. As I hear the band play, I start to lose confidence. This is a bad place to lose confidence. It's like being at the deep end of the pool, putting your foot out, and losing your balance before you realize you can't swim.

And then I hear Johnny say, "Ladies and gentlemen, the always funny Howie Mandel." I've always been very superstitious. I believe you should never utter anything out loud about things you have no control over, or circumstances will turn against you. It drives everyone around me crazy. When I'm driving somewhere and the passenger says, "Wow, the freeway is pretty clear," I snap at the person to shut up for fear I'm about to hit a traffic jam. During a flight, if someone comments, "This is a smooth flight," then we are surely going to experience extreme turbulence. So now I think, Why did he say "always funny"?

The curtain opens, and the audience roars. I can feel the love. I come out pulling a rope attached to a dolly holding the giant saber-toothed tiger. People are laughing and applauding.

When I reach the platform where Johnny's desk is, the tiger's two large front paws won't go up onto the riser. I try to lift the head and pull the tiger toward me, but I can't budge it. I turn to Ed McMahon. "Ed, can you give me a hand?"

This was about forty seconds after I heard "the always funny Howie Mandel." Forty seconds doesn't sound like a lot of time, but in television it's a lifetime. The applause had died down, and all I could hear were murmurs.

Ed stands up. "What do you want me to do?"

"You lift and I'll push," I say. I walk around the back and try to push the tiger onto the riser as Ed pulls. One paw clears the lip of the riser, but not the entire tiger.

I turn to Doc Severinsen and say, "Can you help push?" Doc looks at me strangely, puts down his trumpet, and walks across the stage to the tiger.

So now Doc and I push and Ed pulls. The saber-toothed tiger with the carrot on its back finally lurches up onto the riser, coming to rest directly in front of Johnny, blocking the camera's view of him. Through the earpieces the cameramen are wearing, I can hear the control room barking instructions: "Camera two, camera two, go left." For twenty-five years, they had used the same camera angles, but because I'm there with the saber-toothed tiger and a carrot, the cameras now have to be moved. Things are happening that have never happened before.

Doc and I keep pushing the tiger and Ed keeps pulling. By now I'm sweating. Ed is sweating. Doc is sweating. The entire riser is completely blocked by the thirty-foot tiger. Finally, after about two minutes of maneuvering and sweating in total silence, the tiger is where I believe it should be. Ed sits down, and Doc returns to his place with the band.

I walk around the back of the tiger and sit in the seat next to Johnny, out of breath and covered in sweat. Johnny is just sitting there, tapping his pencil. It's quiet. He looks at me, and I look at him. He says, "Well . . ."

"Well, what?" I reply.

Johnny gestures at this monstrosity sitting in front of him. I have not felt this kind of discomfort in front of an audience since I opened for Diana Ross. Johnny has just asked me, after what seemed like an eternity of horrible silence, to explain what this was. I am fully committed. There's no turning back, so my answer to Johnny is this:

"I don't want to talk about it."

I'll never forget the look on Johnny's face. I thought that was the joke. I truly believed it would be funny to go so far out of my way to set something up and have the payoff be absolutely nothing. That night, I learned that some things look better on paper than when they are actually executed. I told him I would be willing to talk about anything else—family, career, health—but please, I did not want to discuss this, referring to the saber-toothed chaos filling the screens of America's television sets.

After very few uncomfortable exchanges, he turns to the camera and says, "All right, we'll be back with more right after this."

The band plays, and the show goes to commercial. Stage-hands hurry out onstage and remove the giant saber-toothed tiger with the carrot on its back. There is no eye contact between Johnny and me—or me and anyone else, for that matter. We come back from commercial. Remember, right before the commercial Johnny had said that he would be right back with more. Johnny immediately says, "Our next guest is the lovely Connie Stevens," or whoever it was. I guess he didn't mean more of me.

That was that. I was cut off. Later, I was informed by Jim McCawley that I had made Johnny very uncomfortable. I was never invited to do *The Tonight Show* with him again. I continued to appear with Joan Rivers and Garry Shandling when they guest hosted, but never again with Johnny. You know what? I get it. Johnny was the best there has ever been, and he didn't need to feel uncomfortable or be thrown off his game by Howie Mandel arriving with a saber-toothed tiger and a giant carrot.

Looking back, to be honest with you, I realize I did this for the reason I do a lot of things. I did it on impulse, without knowing what was going to happen next. Just like I'm ending this chapter impulsively, without knowing where this book is going next.

ELEVEN

THE FIVE-MILE
RADIUS

For my entire life, my impulsive behavior has known no boundaries—that is, up until now. My tomfoolery—a word I haven't heard since 1962. You know what? Let's change that to monkeyshines. No, make that high jinks. Forget it. My wife has mandated that the stuff I do should not be done within a five-mile radius of where we live.

I cannot tell you in how many places in my neighborhood I'm considered persona non grata. Most of this starts out innocently enough and just ends up evolving into a problem.

If you have ever seen me in public, you will notice I carry a backpack. It's armed with hidden camera equipment. If I get the urge to document my impulsive behavior, I could, number one, entertain myself later, and number two, possibly convince a broadcaster to air these gems on various shows. Many a time you might have seen one on *Regis* or as a "Hidden Howie" piece on *The Tonight Show*. I say "many a time," but the truth is that most of the time they were just for my personal entertainment, never to air.

Here's an example.

It was Halloween, and I wandered into a makeshift costume store. On an impulse, I found the manager, told him who I was, convinced him to let me work behind the counter. I told him that if I was able to capture something with my hidden camera, he could possibly watch it on *The Tonight Show*. This never made it on the air, but if the manager happens to be reading this book and is interested in seeing what we actually captured, come on over to my house. I take that back. My wife is right behind me as I write this and she said, "No, you can't come over."

My first customer was a woman. She asked for a bird costume. I told her to follow me and took her to the back of the store to a large display area.

"What I need you to do is turn around, pull down your pants, pull down your underpants, and bend over," I instructed.

She looked at me as if I were out of my mind. "What are you saying?" she asked.

"What did you ask for?"

"I asked for a bird costume."

"Right, so I need for you to pull down your pants and underpants and bend over," I repeated.

"What are you going to do?"

"Well, I will start with your rear and glue feathers on you," I said very earnestly.

"This is ridiculous," she said. She stared hard at me. "Wait a minute."

"What?"

"Are you Howie Mandel?"

"No, I'm not," I replied. "I work here. Just pull down your pants and let me put feathers on you."

She stared at me, then opened her mouth, and the words that followed were indescribably devastating. "You are Howie Mandel," she insisted. "And I am your daughter Riley's teacher, and you have a parent-teacher conference tonight."

I ripped off my hidden camera glasses and thought, Oh, my God, I just told my daughter's teacher to bend over so I could stick feathers on her ass. I pleaded: "I'm so sorry, I was just trying to do something for *The Tonight Show.* Please, I apologize. I went too far."

The teacher seemed to accept my apology, but I still had to tell my wife. I went home and explained the situation to Terry. Enough was enough. She instituted a five-mile radius: no hidden camera pieces, pranks, or practical jokes within five miles of our home.

She never said anything about *in* the home. There were times that my practical jokes weren't impulsive or funny. Sometimes they were meant to be just practical.

One day when my oldest daughter, Jackie, was just six years old, I took her to a sporting goods store to buy some floaties. She happened to see the camping section and began crawling in and out of the tents. She asked what they were for, and I explained what camping was.

"Daddy, Daddy, I want to go camping with you," she begged. "Please, please, can we go camping?"

When a little girl looks up at you with those saucer eyes, there's no denying her. I agreed to take her camping someday. We bought the floaties and the tent and left. I thought she would think I was a great dad because I had bought a tent and promised to take her camping. Little did I realize that I would have to follow through.

For weeks, she kept asking me when we were going camping. Now, if you know me or you've been paying attention so far, you know that for me, roughing it is checking into a hotel without twenty-four-hour room service. I have enough trouble touching a doorknob in public, much less a piece of wood a squirrel has pissed on.

Finally, I came up with what I thought was a brilliant idea. I told her she could help me set up the tent in the backyard and that night we would go camping . . . in the yard. This way we would be camping, and I could use my own toilet. She was so excited, and I had found a good alternative to roughing it in the wilderness.

We went out into the backyard to build the tent together. It was father-daughter bonding like you've never seen. She was so proud of me. It was four poles and a piece of cloth, but as a Jew, I felt I had really constructed something.

Jackie's bedtime was eight o'clock, which was just after dark. She put on her pajamas. I took a flashlight and a little radio to the tent, and we crawled into our sleeping bags. We started talking about camping. She was mesmerized by everything I had to say for about six minutes, and then she fell asleep at 8:06 p.m.

Now I was lying there quietly in the dark in my backyard. It was a little cold, and honestly, now that she was asleep, it was not fun. So at 8:09 p.m. I came up with a plan.

I jostled her and woke her up. Groggily, she looked up at me. "What, Daddy?"

"It's morning," I told her.

She looked outside. "It can't be, it's still dark."

"When you're camping you get up in the morning before the sun rises," I explained. "That's how you camp."

"But I'm really tired," she said.

"Do you want to go in the house and sleep until the sun comes up?" I asked.

"Okay."

I carried her into her room and tucked her in bed. I then went down to the backyard, packed up the tent, and came back into the house. I tucked myself into my own bed at about ten-thirty p.m.

In Jackie's mind, we had spent an entire night in the wilderness. She thought I was such a hero. She never forgets the time I took her camping and woke her up before the crack of dawn. I never told her the truth. There was no joke, but it was very practical. As I write this, I feel tremendously guilty. I know she will read this book, and that is why I'm confessing. But honey, we did go camping. The only difference between your memory and reality is that in your memory, you went out one night and camped. In reality, you went camping for nine and a half minutes. The important thing is that I love you.

• • •

I feel that I have so much to confess and apologize for. To Riley, for the image that I instilled upon her pre-K teacher. To Jackie, for misleading her and letting her believe that her father was an outdoorsman. And to my son, Alex, for . . . well, let me just tell you the story.

One night when Alex was nine, he noticed a small growth on his chest. I was on the road, and Terry was freaked out. As soon as I came home, we took him to the doctor, who told us that it was nothing to worry about, it was just a calcium deposit.

When I was putting Alex to bed that night, he asked me what the growth was.

Without thinking, words just slipped through my lips. "It's a boner," I said.

"What do you mean?" he asked.

"When you have an extra bone, it's called a boner," I said. "Tomorrow you shouldn't take gym. You should tell them you have a boner, and you can't do gym."

Pretty funny, huh?

I then read him a story and put him to bed. By that time, I had forgotten that I had told him about the boner. The next day, I wasn't home. Terry received a phone call from the teacher. In a very stern voice, the teacher explained that improper language is not tolerated at school and should be discouraged at home. If it persisted, Alex would be suspended. Terry asked exactly what he had said. The teacher told her that Alex was walking around saying that he could not take part in gym class because "my dad said that I have a boner."

Terry quickly figured it out and tried to explain to the teacher that Howie must have been making a joke. The teacher—along with Terry at that moment—didn't share my sense of humor. Yet again, I had acted impulsively, without thinking of the ramifications. My lack of focus distracted me from telling my son this was just a joke before he humiliated himself publicly in school.

While I'm on the subject of public humiliation, I have one more confession. My trusted friend and road manager, Rich Thurber, who has been with me since 1993, was not beyond the sting of my impulsive humor.

As an employee of my company, I bought him health insurance. He doesn't like going to the doctor, but to qualify for the policy, he had to have a physical. In the days leading up to his appointment, he kept asking me if it was required. When I asked what was bothering him, he admitted that he had never had a prostate exam and didn't want to have one. If you open up that can of worms to me, the fun begins.

For those of you who are not aware, a digital prostate exam usually consists of the doctor poking his finger into your ass. That's all I've got. I have no idea what this test actually is or what information he is gleaning. All I know is that I've been in a room with a man who puts his finger in my ass, pulls it out, and tells me I'm okay. If you see me in public, don't ask me how I am. Apparently, the only way to find out is by inserting your finger in my ass. The thought of this was terrifying Rich.

On the day of his appointment, he was visibly nervous. He

asked me again about the prostate exam. "Everyone does it," I assured him. "It's not that bad. What's the worst thing that could happen, a hangnail?"

As soon as Rich left the office for the physical, I called the doctor, whose name and phone number I found on the insurance forms. I told the receptionist that my name was Rich Thurber. "This is very embarrassing for me, but I've never had a prostate exam," I said. "Is it part of the insurance physical?"

She went to check with the doctor and came back on the phone. "Yes, Mr. Thurber, it's required," she said.

"Let me be honest," I told her. "I'm very uncomfortable with that. There is one way I could be made more comfortable. I need to have more people in the room. This is going to sound ridiculous, but if there are at least four or five people there, I would feel more comfortable."

The nurse listened intently. "That's not really standard procedure," she said.

"Please, I will be there in five minutes," I said. "I'm too embarrassed to discuss this in person, and when I get there, I'm not going to mention this request again. I'll act like it never even happened. I hope you understand."

"Sir, I understand," she said. "That's your request, and we will do our best."

I hung up the phone. Having had many prostate exams in my life, I'm aware of how uncomfortable they are physically and mentally. I can't imagine what it would be like if four or five people were spectating. I do not know exactly what happened when Rich got there. He and I never spoke of it again.

I can assure you, whatever happened was uncomfortable for everyone involved. I would like to take this moment to apologize profusely.

I personally like the pranks that take a long time to come to fruition. I love planting a seed or giving out a piece of misinformation that escalates and pays off years later. And even though I'm a professional, one of the greatest examples of this actually happened *to* me.

It was my fiftieth birthday party, and all my friends met at a local restaurant to celebrate. At the end of the evening, Michael Rotenberg, my lifelong friend and manager, gave me an envelope and a picture that revealed something incredibly shocking to me.

Twenty years earlier, Terry and I had bought our first house. Michael and a group of friends, including Lou Dinos and Mark Blutman, had all pitched in and bought me a house-warming/birthday present with a unique story behind it.

Michael explained that they had all gone to the Beverly Hills Art Festival. While there, they ended up meeting the artist who painted the festival's winning picture. This seemed like a unique opportunity. My friends all chipped in to buy it.

The painting was titled *Seasons*. To say that the painting was abstract would be an understatement. Michael gave me a dissertation on how the four seasons were depicted in the painting. I looked at it closely after he described it, and I swear to you, I saw winter, spring, summer, and fall. Because it was such a great gesture from my closest friends, I hung it in a very prominent place in my new home.

When Terry and I bought our next house, I was doing well enough to afford a decorator. He came to our house for a meeting and saw *Seasons* on the wall. The expression on his face was as if someone farted. "You're not taking this, are you?" he asked. I told him it was one of the few things we *were* taking.

I'll tell you, a tinge of hurt came over me. Not only was it a prize-winning painting, but more important, my closest friends had spent their hard-earned money to buy it. At the same time, I'm thinking, We're paying big money for this so-called decorator who can't identify a masterpiece when he sees one. Acting as an art aficionado, I proudly pointed out winter, spring, summer, and fall, just as it had been shown to me. He told me that he saw it, too. I didn't believe him, but I was the customer. He put it in my new house.

Each time we moved over the years, we used the same decorator. I believed that because he had been made aware of the sentimental value *Seasons* held for me, not to mention its well-earned position in the art world, he always made a place for it. As I write this book, I now live in my fourth house since the painting was bestowed upon us. Our decorator delicately informed us that he couldn't think of a place in this house that would showcase our treasure.

So we grudgingly decided to part with *Seasons*. My wife donated it to a local child care facility, where it was prominently displayed above a plaque. That plaque reads: "Donated from the collection of Howie and Terry Mandel. *Seasons*, winner of the 1985 Beverly Hills Art Festival."

Jump ahead to my fiftieth birthday party. Michael hands me an envelope and says, "Here are some pictures from twenty years ago." I open the envelope and cannot believe what I am seeing. There are pictures of all my friends, drinking beer, laughing their asses off, and haphazardly throwing paint on a canvas, creating *Seasons*. It looked like nine special-needs children with a broken spin art.

I'm now fifty-three years old. Three years have passed since the forgery was revealed. It was all a lie, and the painting is actually worthless. But a joke that takes twenty years to come to fruition is priceless.

You might think being the victim for a change would be embarrassing, but it's really hard to embarrass me. In fact, I've been truly embarrassed only twice in my life. Neither of those times involved a practical joke. But both of them involved my daughter Jackie.

She was just about two years old and *almost* finished with the potty-training process. This would be one of the first times that I would take her out on my own. My wife dressed her up and put her in the car seat, and we were off.

As soon as we reached where we were going, my little girl looked at me and said, "I have to go potty."

I hadn't given this any thought. Horror set in because of my issues with public restrooms. I couldn't take her to the ladies' room, and the thought of having my baby sit down in the men's room was even worse. Any public restroom is my living hell. I don't know what's going to happen when I meet my Maker, but if there is a heaven and a hell and I don't get into heaven, they will leave me in a public restroom.

Rather than working something out, I turned to her and said, "Honey, I'm taking you home. You are going to go potty at home."

She said, "I'm going to make here."

"Please hold it," I pleaded.

I picked her up, ran like the wind to my car, strapped her into her seat, and started home. I was speeding down the Ventura Freeway when I heard another sound from the car seat behind me. "Daddy, I'm going to go."

"Please don't go, we are almost home," I begged.

"I can't hold it."

"Okay, I'm going to pull off and go to a gas station."

"I can't hold it, I'm going to go now."

Desperately, I said, "Forget the gas station. I'm stopping right here."

I whipped the car over to the soft shoulder of the freeway. There were hedges all along the freeway, so I figured I could take her behind them. I ran around the car, picked Jackie up and carried her into the hedges. As I broke into the greenery, lo and behold, the ground disappeared from under my feet—it was a ravine.

I fell flat on my back and began to plummet. As I fell, I tried to protect my baby by cradling her in my arms. I could hear the breaking of twigs and I could feel my pants ripping and the branches scraping my skin. Jackie began to scream, and I yelled, "It's okay, baby! It's okay!"

I kept sliding down, down, down, until I finally came to a stop in a mucky—I hoped it was muck—swampy cesspool of a puddle. I stood up, and with the baby still in my arms, I looked down at my mud-caked, ripped pants and bleeding legs. She was screaming and crying and still saying, "Daddy, I have to go!"

Terry had dressed her in a jumpsuit that was now dirtied by our fall. I gingerly unbuttoned it and pulled it down around her ankles. I held her out at arm's length and said, "Go ahead and make."

"I can't," she said. "I'm going to make on my pants." As if that could make this situation any worse.

A brilliant thought crossed my mind. I would continue to hold her out in front of me. I would have her put her feet up on my shoulders; that way, she could pee straight down onto the ground. Apparently, however, the dynamics of female urination are not my strong suit. Before I could finish saying the word *go,* she began to pee. A fire hose of urine spewed directly into my face. I began to scream as I tried to shift her position. The stream of piss moved from my eye directly into my mouth. I began to gag. I was about to vomit.

And then all was quiet. I gathered myself. I removed her wet clothes. We just stood there, and I thought, This is why I'm never going to go camping . . . for more than nine minutes. I had swallowed a half-gallon of urine. My legs were bleeding. I was covered in mud—at least I hoped it was mud. The only upside of having a face full of urine was that my little girl couldn't tell I was crying.

"Daddy, I want to go home," she said.

"So do I."

I put her under my arm and began to traverse the hill. As I climbed up, she also became covered in muck—I hoped it was muck. I could barely make my way to the top. The stinging of urine in my eyes. The taste of urine in my mouth. Blood trickling down my legs. And a naked, muddy little girl under my arm.

It seemed like forever, climbing, grabbing at twigs and rocks and branches to steady myself. Finally, I reached the top. I spread the hedges and could see the highway. I can't remember ever being so happy to see the Ventura Freeway at rush hour.

Picture this: You're driving down the freeway when a tattered, disheveled man, soaked in urine, mud, and blood and holding a screaming, naked baby, emerges from the bushes at the side of the road. As I stepped out, a car slowed down and the concerned citizen behind the wheel looked to see what the hell this was. He rolled down the window and made eye contact. I could see a confused glimmer of recognition as he asked, "Aren't you Howie Mandel?"

I screamed, "No!" and he stepped on the gas and drove off. I made my way to the car, put my daughter inside, and drove home, where my wife was waiting on the porch. Needless to say, from that day on, I wasn't allowed to take my daughter beyond a five-mile radius.

My wife had set up these parameters to prevent embarrassing things from happening. But the truth is that I didn't even need to leave my own backyard to be embarrassed.

Let me take you to a different time, same daughter.

We had built a swing set in our yard on a small area of grass separated from our neighbors' pool by tall hedges. Every day I would come home from work and Jackie would say, "Daddy, take me to the swings."

One day when I was out there with my daughter, I could hear the neighbors on the other side talking. It was the first time I realized how close their pool was to the swing set. It seemed as if they were a foot and a half away.

I was trying to show Jackie how to put her hands on the ropes and move her legs so that she could get high in the air on her own power. She was just a little girl and could not master the coordination. I decided to help her.

I got on the swing myself and put her on my lap. I rocked my legs back and forth. Before you knew it, we were swinging. She was giggling and loving every minute. It was a beautiful father-daughter Norman Rockwell image.

I was grunting and pushing, trying to reach the clouds. "Oh, ah! Oh, ah!" I panted.

"Go, Daddy! Go!" she said.

So I grunted harder. "Oh . . . ah . . . oh . . . ah!"

Finally, just as I got my legs up into the clouds, through the ohs and ahs, I said, "Jackie, how does that feel?" I pushed higher and higher. "Oh, ah! Oh, ah!"

In the midst of the pushing and the grunting and the ohs and the ahs, Jackie said something I believe the neighbors will never forget: "Daddy, I can feel your penis on my butt."

My entire being filled with horror. I immediately realized why the neighbors had stopped talking. As fast as I could, I jammed my heels into the dirt and brought the swing to an immediate halt. I grabbed Jackie and ran into the house. I can only imagine the sick and twisted image the neighbors had of my child rearing, no pun intended.

From that point on, the neighbors wouldn't even make eye

contact with me. They eventually sold the house and moved away. I guess the sound of a grown man grunting and moaning, "Oh, ah!" and a little girl saying, "Daddy, I can feel your penis on my butt," is really hard to explain. As I sit here and write this, you can't imagine how embarrassing it was to me. And this is one of those moments that make me not want to do anything within a five-mile radius of myself.

UH-OH, IT'S WORSE

As I sit here writing, I should feel that the odds of surviving to finish this book are better because my heart rate is being monitored. The truth is that the heart monitor makes everything worse. My whole life is about distraction. Now I've got all this tape on my nipple and wires running inside my shirt. Just being aware of this makes my heart rate go up.

Because I talk about this problem so much in the press, a medical company has sent me a defibrillator. What am I supposed to do with a carry-on defibrillator? If my heart stops and I pass out, how am I supposed to defibrillate myself? I made my road manager, Rich Thurber, read the manual so that if anything happens, he can defibrillate me. If you see me lying unconscious someplace, please try to find Rich Thurber.

I have been getting progressively worse. Even though my medication has been changed twice, my heart rate fluctuates continuously. I can't breathe, and I'm dizzy. My whole goal in life now is just trying not to pass out. The monitor actually rang in the middle of a live performance. I was forced to explain to the audience that the ringing sound was my heart monitor. "What you are witnessing is a medical emergency." Their response was laughter. "No, really, I'm dying here, people." They laughed again. I guess in comedy, nobody can hear you scream.

The next day, I flew home and went to the doctor. He decided that the medication was not working and the only answer, as he had suspected right from the beginning, was the ablation. The date was set: May 21, 2009.

A group of strangers are going to make their way through my crotch to my heart armed only with a camera and a laser. Dr. Cannom is trying to comfort me by telling me that I have a flutter. This is not comforting, it's just confusing. He explained to me that the flutter, which occurs on the right side of the heart, can instigate the high heart rate and the afib. If he just zaps the flutter, all will be cured. Even though they will still be slicing my loins to get to the main event, they will only have to torch the right side of my heart. Oh, what a relief?

I'm not kidding you when I say I don't believe I will survive to that date. At this point, I feel as if my body is taking in the minimum amount of oxygen. It's the most physically uncomfortable I have ever been. I'm dizzy and weak. I want to pass out. It feels as if I am drowning.

The show must go on. If you witnessed any of the performances at this particular time, you might have noticed I was much less hyper than usual—though the adrenaline rush that accompanies performance anxiety helped to fuel me through each show. It was just like my showcase for Joan Rivers with a 103-degree fever. I began to refer to these shows as my farewell tour.

I'm writing this at the end of the day. I'm thrilled to say another day and I didn't die. But there's always May 21.

TWELVE

SHIT
HAPPENS

I now realize that neither my career nor my life has been about blazing a trail. I'm just wandering along a path, and every so often shit happens. And I don't mean shit in a derogatory sense. From the moment I walked onstage at Yuk Yuk's to the day I moved to Los Angeles to the reading I did for Brandon Tartikoff, I was always cognizant of being in a place I didn't plan on being.

One of those reflective moments happened in New York in October 1987. I had sold out two shows on the same night at Radio City Music Hall. After the first show, I went up to my dressing room and looked out the window onto Sixth Avenue. I'll never forget that image. It was unbelievable. Barricades had been set up, and the police were handling traffic control.

I was looking at a mass of humanity clogging the streets of midtown Manhattan whose only reason for being there was Howie Mandel. Seven thousand people were pouring out into the street, leaving the first show, as another seven thousand people were trying to get in for my next performance.

Every experience up to that point had been wonderfully and indescribably surreal. Less than a decade and a half earlier, I had been sitting alone in a Howard Johnson's at one a.m., trying to get a few strangers to laugh at my vagina routine. Now fourteen thousand fans were paying to see me at the storied Radio City Music Hall. Even my personal life seemed surreal. I was now the father of a little girl. It was hard to fathom that the irresponsible carpet salesman who would lie shirtless on the floor and creep out customers was now somebody's dad.

St. Elsewhere was in the midst of its critical and commercial success, I was doing two hundred sold-out concert dates a year, and I had begun to star in films. I had the opportunity to appear in *A Fine Mess*, directed and produced by Blake Edwards, the legendary filmmaker of the Pink Panther movies, *Victor Victoria*, and *10*. Though I don't believe the film made anyone's top ten list, it was a great experience for me.

One day in a quiet moment, Blake told me a story that touched me in a way I just can't shake. It was the story of a man who was in his therapist's office, curled up in the fetal position, in the deepest and darkest of depressions. He had been crying inconsolably for weeks, and every muscle in his body ached with anguish. The therapist was at her wits' end. She had used every tool in the arsenal of the psychiatric and medical community to rescue this man from the depths of his misery. Cognitive therapy had not worked. Meds had not worked. She was bent on not losing the battle with his living hell. Alas, she was about to recommend the most powerful tool to rescue this man from his agonizing desperation: laughter. Laughter, after all, is the best medicine.

The therapist had read the paper that morning and seen an ad for the circus, which had been in town for two weeks. The last show was that night. The featured act was Socko the Clown. He was renowned for being able to make anyone laugh at any time. No one who witnessed Socko for even a moment could keep from laughing. He was the living embodiment of laughter. She figured if this man could experience even a single moment, he would be pulled back from the brink. What were the chances that she would see the paper on the final night? She was sure luck was on his side. The therapist was thrilled to announce, "I have the solution. I know this will work. Tonight, I will take you to see Socko the Clown." The man slowly lifted his head and looked up at the therapist. With tears streaming down his cheeks, in the most agonizing voice, he revealed, "I *am* Socko the Clown."

This story turned out to be eleven times better than the film. But in Hollywood, you are only as successful as people think you might be, so even before *A Fine Mess* was released, I was offered a deal at MGM. This yielded my next cinematic treat: *Walk Like a Man*, a film depicting a boy raised by wolves. I can't tell you how many endless afternoons director Mel Frank wanted to rehearse with me. He would bring me to his house in Brentwood and have me crawl on all fours. Frustrated with my progress, he had the studio hire a trainer to help my technique.

During my Christmas vacation, MGM sent a trainer to Waikiki, Hawaii, to work with me. Every day at the Sheraton Waikiki when I came up from the pool in the afternoon, this woman would make me run up and down the halls on all fours, forty or fifty times. As embarrassing as it was, I thought, Oh, my God, I'm a movie star.

I thought this must be the Method training that actors went on talk shows to discuss. They would tell stories about how they gained fifty pounds or grew their hair long and didn't shower for a week to get in character. I was crawling in the hallways to become Bobo the dog-boy.

They hired Christopher Lloyd to play my brother just after *Back to the Future* was released. They cast Cloris Leachman to play my mom. Everybody was on board, but it just never felt right to me.

I've never been the same since *Walk Like a Man*. To this day, my back hurts from crawling around on all fours for three months. In one particular scene, Christopher Lloyd was supposed to pull a bone out of my mouth on the count of three. I'll write it one more time: on the count of *three*. Not two. As the director got to two, Christopher pulled with all his might. I felt a crazy-ass pain as I heard a snap reverberate throughout my head. If you happen to see the movie today, during the dinner scene when he pulls the bone out of my mouth, it looks as though a piece of meat is flying in the air. That is not meat. That is my front tooth.

After that film, I did *Little Monsters* with Fred Savage of *Wonder Years* fame. I lived for three months over a summer in Wilmington, North Carolina, with ninety-degree heat and 90 percent humidity. To make matters worse, I played a monster. I would arrive at four a.m. and undergo five hours of makeup. They adhered latex to every inch of my exposed skin. Now I know what it feels like to be a penis wearing a condom on a hot summer night.

Not every film was as physically demanding. The easiest to date has to be *Gremlins*. I happened to land the voice of Gizmo. He's the little fuzzy creature that starts the whole thing. All I had to do was spend a couple of weeks in an air-conditioned sound booth, without any makeup, making ridiculous sounds.

To this day, people will approach me and say, "I loved the Gizmo voice." I'm not trying to burst their bubble when I tell them that the Gizmo sound is the same sound I use for Bobby in *Bobby's World*. Not to drag it down any further, but the Bobby voice is the same sound I used for Skeeter on *Muppet Babies*. It's not as if I don't have a vast array of sounds. I was also Bunsen Honeydoo and Animal on *Muppet Babies*.

I eventually started to turn down roles. It was so hard for me to relinquish control and sit on set for three months and then wait another six months for an audience reaction. Eventually, film offers stopped coming my way. I can say with near certainty that there will never be a Howie Mandel Film Festival.

By the end of the 1980s, I had sold out comedy concerts, done dramatic acting on a critically acclaimed medical series, and starred in various motion pictures. And now once again, another turn. I was approached by two old friends, Jim Staahl and Jim Fisher, who had a deal at Fox Kids Network. They wanted to develop the Bobby character into a Saturday morning cartoon series.

Up until now, Bobby was a voice I was doing at the foot of my parents' bed and a vulgar-spewing little boy in my stand-up act. I had no idea how to hone this into a program for kids. Purely out of a lack of ideas, we started talking about things that happened to us in childhood and to our own children. These stories became the background for the show. *Bobby's World* was eventually nominated for Emmys, was syndicated worldwide, and became a Happy Meal. Wow, shit happens.

Nobody was more excited about my career than my father. When I was shooting on set, he would fly to L.A. and hang out on the soundstage of *St. Elsewhere* or any movie I was doing. He also loved being on the road. When I toured, he would fly to my shows. He'd stand in the wings, always laughing no matter how many times he had heard the same routine. If I was featured in a small article in *People,* he would go into every 7-Eleven and open the magazine to the page with me on it. I felt as though all of it—every performance, my entire career—was just for my dad. I had come a long way from standing at the end of his bed trying to make him giggle.

One day in January 1989, my mother called me in tears. "I think there is something definitely wrong with your father," she said.

My heart dropped.

My father, who had been a smoker until five years earlier, had a cough that wouldn't go away, so he went to our family doctor. He got an "uh-oh." The doctor sent him for a lung X-ray. When my parents called for the results, the doctor asked them to come in for a meeting. They both knew that it was a bad sign if they couldn't get the results over the phone.

I tried to put on an optimistic face. I told my mom that we didn't know what the results were and that I would fly in and meet the doctor with them. I got to Toronto the next day and went directly to the doctor's office.

We were sitting in the waiting room. I excused myself to go to the bathroom. Without my parents knowing, I went into the doctor's office and told him that I was Albert Mandel's son. I asked him what he had seen on the X-ray. He said that my father had inoperable lung cancer. The doctor then informed me that my father had no more than one month to live. There couldn't have been a more dire diagnosis. Those words shook me to my core.

"Okay, I'm going to get down on my knees and beg," I said to the doctor. "You cannot tell them that he has one month to live."

"What?" he said.

"You cannot tell them," I repeated. "Don't lie, but avoid telling him he's dying."

"I don't believe in that," he said.

"I do."

I believe the only thing that can help people through tough times is hope. If they are going to die, they are going to die anyway. They die the moment you tell them, because they lose hope. People always say, "You have to get your affairs in order." I don't know what that means. Maybe that's because I don't care about material things. What's important to me is the quality of life right to the end.

I begged the doctor not to tell them. I think the fact that he had seen me on TV playing a doctor helped, because he finally agreed that only if they didn't ask directly, he would not deliver the death sentence.

I returned to the waiting room. It was the hardest acting I've ever had to do. In the face of the worst news I had ever heard in my life, I regained my composure and sat back down next to my parents. They had always been there for me. Now, for the first time in my life, I was trying to be there for them.

They didn't know I had gone into the doctor's office. My mom asked what took so long. I told her some lame joke about having a bladder infection because it wouldn't come out. I made a few more jokes. They were the hardest jokes I have ever made, and they weren't the least bit funny. I was just trying to act as though I hadn't heard what I'd just heard.

When the receptionist called my father, we all went into the office where I had just met with the doctor. Very professionally, he clipped my father's X-rays to the backlit wall. No layman could conclude anything by looking at them.

The doctor measured his words. "How do you feel?" he asked my father, who responded that he was congested. The doctor nodded and took out his prescription pad. "I'm going to prescribe these pills, which may open up your airways," he said. "If you take this pill, you should feel better." My mother and father were both too scared of the answer to ask the question. I knew the doctor wouldn't lie and that if they had asked if it was cancer, he would've had to say yes.

The fact that he had told my father to take some pills to help his breathing made all the difference in the world. When my parents walked out of that office, my father had a little hop in his step even though he was coughing and could barely breathe. They had obviously expected the worst and now with no mention of cancer had a glimmer of hope.

We got in the car and drove to Max Milk, a convenience store. My father bought a lottery ticket. Nothing says hope and future like a lottery ticket. We went home. He clearly didn't feel well, but he hadn't been given a death sentence.

My feeling is that what you don't know doesn't bother you. I've never believed more in my life that ignorance is bliss. We all know we are going to die. I don't need to know when. I don't need a date. I couldn't live knowing when I was going to die. There are a lot of people who think it's better to know all the details, and I respect that. But it seems that everybody should call that for themselves, instead of a doctor making that decision for them.

My father became progressively sicker. Ten days later, he was hospitalized. I took him to the ER and admitted him. They checked him into a room and helped him undress and put on a hospital gown. They gave him a plastic bag for his belongings, sweatpants, shirt, and glasses. To this day, I have that bag on a shelf in my bedroom.

My mom and I went home that night from the hospital, and I told her the prognosis. I'm pretty sure that she already knew, but not having heard it from the doctor, she hadn't been forced to face it.

Lung cancer is a cruel disease, and for the next three

weeks, I witnessed the most harrowing things happen to my father. It was like watching somebody slowly drown or choke to death. I can't think of anything more horrific. I was in his room at his bedside, and I watched him die. It was horrible. There aren't words to describe that feeling.

My father was gone, and it was so hard to fathom that I would never see my dad again. I now believe in the afterlife, but I didn't up until that moment. Even on a scientific level, energy cannot be destroyed, it can only change form. There is no more tactile an energy than the life force.

I don't know if you've ever sat in a quiet room at a desk doing work and felt that somebody was watching you. There wasn't a noise, you just had a sense, and I'm not talking about sound or sight. You turn around and there is a person there. You didn't hear or smell that person; you just felt his life energy.

When my father was pronounced dead, I had a feeling that he was still there. He wasn't in his body, but he was in the room. Four or five minutes had passed. The nurses were disconnecting various medical machines from the body. Impulsively, for reasons I can't explain, I screamed, "Dad, please, Dad!" at some entity I felt in the room. I sensed that energy come back down into his body, and then he took one more huge gasp and released. Everyone in the room was taken aback, because he had been pronounced dead minutes earlier. He was gone, but from that moment on, I have always felt he is constantly with me.

I had never even been to a funeral, and now I had to help arrange one. I was amazed at how things were all taken care of in a very businesslike manner. The funeral home director began telling me what I would need. In the Jewish religion, we sit shiva, which is a seven-day period of mourning. There are certain rituals involved in this, and everything needed was available for rent from the funeral home. Most people probably find that convenient, but I found it really strange.

The mortician made his pitch. "People will come to your apartment to visit you after the burial, so for twelve dollars a week you can rent a big plastic container where people can put their boots," he explained. "For an extra sixteen dollars, we can include a coatrack."

This is not a bad thing, but it truly is a little like a used-car lot. I'm not knocking the mortician, because he is providing a service. I just find shopping for coffins weird. It's a wooden box that goes into the ground, never to be seen again. There was one with a Star of David on top and another with brass hinges for an extra $300—does it really matter?

After we buried my father, we returned to my parents' apartment to sit shiva. As is customary, friends send trays of food to comfort and feed the mourning family. They had worked out a schedule between them: "You take lunch on Tuesday, I will handle Wednesday." Each day, we thanked the people who brought the trays and then spent the rest of the afternoon talking about how great the lox was. "His death was terrible, but you know something, this fish is tremendous."

For seven days, there was a constant flow of people in and out of the apartment paying their respects. On one particular afternoon, an elderly man approached me and asked if I was the son. I said that I was.

"Can I just say your father was a great man," he said.

"Thank you very much, sir," I said.

"I'll never forget your father up on that hill in Acapulco," the man said. "Boy, could he sing."

I nodded politely until I realized what he had said. "My father didn't sing."

"What?" he asked.

"I don't think my father sang, and I don't remember him going to Acapulco."

The man looked confused and then asked, "Is this the Levinson shiva?"

"No, that's on the sixth floor," I said.

"Please excuse me," he said.

Instead of leaving, he made his way over to the fish platter, took another serving, wrapped it in a napkin, and then left for the Levinson affair.

On shiva day four, a man my father's age approached.

"You're Howie," he said.

"Yes," I said.

"I was good friends with your father, and I just want to say he will be sorely missed."

I was about to say, "Nice to meet you," but all I got out was "Nice to—" as he then turned on a dime and ran out of the apartment. I wasn't sure what had happened or if I had done something wrong.

As he was running toward the door, I noticed that he had dropped something. It looked like a piece of candy in a shiny cellophane wrapper. I bent down to pick it up. As I touched it, my fingers sank into the candy. I held it closer to my face to smell the substance. It hit me: Oh, my God, it's shit! This guy just shit his pants. The turd had dropped down his pant leg onto our living room carpet. As bad as that might sound, it was much worse. This man's shit was now all over my fingers. I couldn't talk. I couldn't breathe. I just began to scream.

My mom rushed to my side. "What's wrong? What's wrong?"

I couldn't get the words out of my mouth. "There's sh . . . sh . . . shit on my hands!"

"What happened?" she asked.

"That man, that man shit on the carpet," I managed to say.

She held my hand away from my body and led me into the bathroom like a two-year-old. She turned on scalding water and put my hands under the faucet. She went to the bar in the living room and grabbed the vodka and tequila and whatever other alcohol was available. She then came back into the bathroom and doused my hands with the liquor. I was screaming, and so was she.

"Oh, my God! Oh, my God!" I wailed.

"Please, please, Howie, calm down," she said.

The mourners in the other room were listening to us wailing, thinking that we had been overcome by grief. I *was* devastated. Talk about a bad week. I had just buried my father, which made me feel like a piece of shit—and now to make matters worse, on my fingers was an actual piece of shit. I guess shit happens.

THIRTEEN

STAND-UP AND BE COUNTED

So many things personal and professional continuously change in one's life. My one constant has been stand-up. From that moment on April 19, 1978, when I took the stage at Yuk Yuk's, I realized that my comfort zone was standing onstage behind a mike with a light shining on me. Many people in show business use stand-up as a stepping-stone to other things, whether it's movies, TV series, directing, or hosting a late-night talk show. Jim Carrey, David Letterman, and Mike Nichols are just a few examples. Once they find success in that new field, they abandon stand-up. For me, whether I was in the midst of *St. Elsewhere*, filming a movie, or creating *Bobby's World*, my real home continued to be onstage.

I can remember only one time where it didn't feel right. That was after the loss of my father, which was the darkest moment of my life. I can remember my first time back onstage. The introduction might as well have been, "Ladies and gentlemen, Socko the Clown." I certainly didn't feel funny. Being silly and making a few thousand strangers laugh felt somewhat awkward. I would look to the wings and search for my father. Not seeing him standing there watching me was even more devastating. It felt so wrong, but I had obligations to meet.

In the Jewish religion, it is traditional to say a prayer before sundown each and every night for a year to commemorate the memory of the deceased. This prayer is to be done with at least ten men. I had never been that observant, but I wanted to show respect for my father. I had it written into my contract that no concert would start before sundown, and the promoter was to find me a group of ten Jewish men for my prayer service. Was this too much to ask? Apparently, yes.

The problem was that in many of the small midwestern towns, there were no synagogues and very few Jews. When a promoter couldn't find ten Jews for me to pray with, he would check the death notices in the local paper, pick me up at the airport, and drive me to a funeral of strangers. I would ask if they minded if I prayed with them before I went off and did my comedy show.

Eventually, I worked my way back into feeling comfortably uncomfortable onstage. The discomfort of which I speak is the all-encompassing fear I crave. The fear that drew me to this career. The fear of not knowing what's going to happen next. The fear of not being accepted by the audience. You might ask yourself, "Why would any human subject himself to this?"

My analogy has always been of a roller coaster. I happen to love roller coasters. If I rode a roller coaster that glided smoothly past a couple of trees, I would probably never go on it again. On the other hand, the scarier it is, the closer you think you are coming to death, the more physically uncomfortable it is, the more fun the ride is. That's exactly how I felt the first night onstage at Yuk Yuk's. That's the feeling I've chased every night since. I continually wanted to get back on that roller coaster. Fear is my fuel.

I've read some self-help books like *The Power of Now* by Eckhart Tolle. The basic philosophy of this book is that all of us live either in the past or in the future. We make our decisions based on what has happened or what might happen. You make the decision not to show up at a party for fear an ex-girlfriend might be there. Or you avoid the party because last time it was boring. Just because the party was boring last time doesn't mean it won't be fun this time, and the ex may never show up. If you base your decision on these thoughts, the only guarantee is that you will miss the party and the opportunity to meet someone who could end up being a positive in your life.

As an anxiety-ridden victim of OCD, on any given day you may find me in my hotel room spreading towels so my feet won't touch the carpet out of fear of what might get on them in the minutes to come. I could be scalding myself in the shower to wash off the germs I believe I've picked up in the past hour. If I could just focus on the now, I might realize I'm okay. The only place that I've found the ability to do this is on-stage. Every other issue seems to disappear as I live in the moment of performance.

A perfect example of this was my audition for *The Tonight Show* in front of Joan Rivers. I was so sick that I believed my future was certain death—until the moment I hit the stage. Then all was forgotten. The adrenaline rushed, and I delivered. But the moment I said good night and walked off the stage, the shadow of death was back upon me.

This is the reason a good portion of my act is improvised. I do have set material, but what I love is when an audience member or a happening takes me off that beaten path. I would love the microphone to go dead. I would love the lights to go out. I would love for somebody to scream or come toward the stage. My shows are like my interactive thrill ride. I will not let myself be complacent or comfortable. I can't tell you how exciting it is to me to have these happenings force me into the now.

To this end, I have no preparations or rituals when it comes to stand-up. There are times when I'm talking to somebody prior to a show in my dressing room. The stage manager will alert me that we will begin in five minutes. Inevitably, the person I'm with will say, "I'll give you a couple minutes alone." That's the worst thing you can do to me. I have nothing to do, and I don't want any more time with myself. I really don't. All the distractions I look for in life are about trying to get away from myself. And then the moment I crave: I hear my tour manager, Rich, announce, "Ladies and gentlemen, Howie Mandel!" The lights go up and I am enveloped in fear.

As much as I use this fear as a glorious distraction, there are times this discomfort does not serve me. I could be standing in front of an audience of five thousand people who are roaring with laughter. If I happen to notice one person who is not being entertained, my whole evening becomes about that one guy. Every thought, every joke, every gag, is now directed at him. I forget the entire audience, and in my mind I put myself back on *Make Me Laugh*. The other 4,999 people can give me a standing ovation, yet all I can think about is the one guy who didn't seem to like me.

I consider my performances giant parties with me just trying to be the center of attention. I want all eyes focused on me, all the time.

One particular night, I had two thousand people in the palm of my hands—except for one man in the front row just off to my left. He seemed to refuse even to look at me. He would look everywhere but at me—left, right, up, down. It was as if someone had dragged him to this concert and he couldn't wait to leave. The rest of the audience was hanging on my every word, convulsing with laughter. Finally and impulsively, I exploded into the *now*.

At this moment, no thought of the past or the future existed. Past: The audience had been laughing for the last hour. Future: What I was about to do could derail the entire show. I could not hold myself back. I didn't have any funny place to go. I just had to get it off my chest.

I said to the audience: "Can I tell you something? This guy

sitting in the front row is not paying any attention. He hasn't looked at me once." I pointed to him. "What the hell is your problem?"

Everyone was laughing in anticipation of where I might be going with the discomfort I was imposing on this poor man. When I end up doing things like this, my mind becomes a blank slate. In no way could I possibly anticipate what his answer would be, or my response.

The man just sat there, continued to look away, and did not say anything.

I demanded, "Sir, you with the red shirt, I'm talking to *you.*"

Now the audience grew quiet, waiting apprehensively for his response. Finally, like a knife piercing through the silence, the woman sitting beside him screamed, "He's blind."

Oh, my God. You could hear a collective gasp from the audience. A little piece of me died in that moment. I've never seen humor get sucked out of a room faster. It was like death. I thought, Where do I go from here? I like unpredictable, but this was crazy. I could feel my heart in my underpants—at least I think it was my heart.

I've always believed honesty is the best policy. "Ladies and gentlemen," I started, hoping to work my way past the embarrassment, "you have just witnessed a huge mistake in comedy, and I'm going to be totally honest with you, I don't know how to get out of this. You've enjoyed the show up until this moment. I hope you've gotten your money's worth, because I don't know where it's going from here."

The audience seemed very uneasy, and so was I. Then I thought, I'm already in the shithouse, I might as well ask what

I'm thinking. Again, pure honesty coupled with impulsiveness. I directed my questioning back to the blind man.

"Sir, I am so sorry. I had no idea you were blind."

He responded, "That's okay."

"But I have one question for you."

You could feel the nervous tension building in the room. Here comes the question: "Why the fuck does a blind man need front-row seats?"

The audience exploded with laughter, along with the blind man. Whew! I had been pulled back from the brink. I continued to the woman he was with: "You should've saved your money and bought the cheaper balcony seats and just told him he was in the front row."

Those are some of my favorite moments in performance. The audience senses the electricity, an invisible feeling that what is happening now is dangerous, has never happened before, and is never going to happen again. That is the power of now. There is something perversely entertaining about seeing a comedian in trouble. This relates to my interpretation of a sense of humor. If somebody is in trouble and flailing, you've got to find the funny there. I use finding the funny as a coping skill in life.

Throughout the 1990s, I continued to sell out huge venues and multiple shows, some of which were documented on various cable specials. I did *Howie Mandel on Ice* for HBO and *Howie Spent Our Summer* for Showtime. After *St. Elsewhere* finished its six-year run, I did about seven pilots for TV shows that never came to fruition.

But then in 1996, Michael Gelman, the executive producer of *Live with Regis and Kathie Lee*, started calling and asking me to fill in for Regis. Michael is the consummate producer. It's probably one of the few shows I've ever done where I didn't need any preparation. The guests were booked. If there was going to be any business, it was all preset. I could show up fifteen minutes before the show, powder my forehead, and go on the air. It was such an easy gig. I had a funny repartee with Kathie Lee. She was straitlaced, and I was a crazy comedian.

Michael also knew I liked to prank people, so he suggested we do it on the show. He was the one who gave me a pair of hidden camera glasses and sent me out into the world.

One piece I remember in particular was when they took me to the Empire State Building and outfitted me as a tour guide. I waited until a family who had been standing in line for three hours reached the front. I could see the anticipation in their faces at the prospect of seeing the New York City skyline from the tallest building. I escorted them into the elevator as the tour from hell began.

Within the small confines of the elevator, I took out a megaphone and began reading word for word the official tourist pamphlet. My volume was deafening, to say the least. The elevator stopped and I led them out. The tourists seemed somewhat confused. That confusion might have been due to the fact that this was the second floor. You could see the dismay on their faces as they looked out the window at the heads of passersby on the street below.

Ever so meekly, the father said, "We came all the way from Des Moines. Can't we go to the top?"

"Not today," I said. "Now, please let me continue with the rich history of this man-made wonder."

I would go on for twenty minutes. People were so polite. They wouldn't interrupt. They would just stand there disappointed. At the end, we revealed that it was a prank and sent them back to the end of the line so they could get a real ride to the top. No, I'm not that mean, people. Off camera, they were escorted directly to the top for free without me.

My appearances on *Regis* were so well received that I began to get offers to host my own daytime show. This was just another opportunity happening to me. So let's do a recap of my professional life up to this point: carpet salesman, comedian, television and movie actor, Saturday morning cartoon, and now daytime talk show host.

I ended up making a deal with Paramount Television. The people there could not have been more supportive and excited about me. I had never been in a position where the producers served my every whim. The first thing I requested was to move into the old *Tonight Show* studio. Jay Leno had taken over from Johnny Carson and moved to the stage across the hall. I wanted to put my desk exactly where Johnny Carson had his. Paramount made it happen.

The first day we took over the studio, I walked under the bleachers and found the cue cards from Johnny Carson's final broadcast. There were cards for Johnny's monologue, as well as introductions for Robin Williams and Bette Midler. The stagehands apparently had just thrown them down and walked out at the end of the night. I still have them.

I signed the deal one year before the show premiered and then traveled to the different markets to meet with all the local stations. Whenever I was in L.A., I would go to the carpenter shop and watch them work on my set. I would marvel, *They're building this palace for me.* It was all for *The Howie Mandel Show.* I felt that I had reached another pinnacle.

The show premiered on June 22, 1998. At that particular time, daytime was crowded. *Judge Judy* was raging. *The Rosie O'Donnell Show* was three years into its run, and Rosie was at the top of her game. *Donny & Marie* was on. Roseanne Barr had a talk show. Martin Short was launching his show the following year. And, of course, there was the gold standard, *The Oprah Winfrey Show.* There were five afternoon talk shows airing in the Los Angeles market alone.

As tough as that sounds, the marketing geniuses felt that they could position me as "the only solo male hosting a talk/variety show on daytime television." Weeks before my actual launch, they made the following pitch to the industry:

Howie Mandel
has a trio of strategic advantages:

1. HOWIE has a three-month "jump start" on the fall crop of daytime competition.

2. HOWIE will serve up fresh new shows during the summer "rerun season" of other programs.

3. HOWIE can stake out a leadership position and build an audience at a time of the year viewers aren't deluged with dozens of new shows.

---

4. HOWIE was canceled after one year.

We were actually canceled at the exact same rating we had when we launched. The good news was that we never lost a viewer. The bad news was that we never gained any viewers.

I think the talk show also changed my persona in the public's mind. Before the show, I had been doing two hundred stand-up shows a year to sold-out audiences. But because I had been on afternoon television hosting a soft-sell show, ticket sales were cut in half. Instead of coming off as a subversive, edgy comedian, I was a guy in your house every day doing light afternoon chitchat. I was the guy talking to soap opera stars and supervising makeovers.

A few years earlier, I was playing in front of fourteen thousand people at Radio City Music Hall. Now I was playing in a small midwestern town in front of fifteen hundred people. I could actually see the face of the last person in the last row.

It felt as if my career were ending. I was literally watching my audience disappear. The one constant I had was my stand-up comedy. Up until now, that part of my career had consistently grown. Now it was drying up. I thought, The next step for me will be playing clubs. But then when the clubs don't want me, what will I do? I did not want to quit the business, but the business was quitting me.

FOURTEEN

HERE'S THE
DEAL

After the cancellation of my talk show, I became depressed. I couldn't get excited about anything in my career or my life. I booked more stand-up dates just to keep busy. It was the Socko the Clown Summer Tour. I was playing small venues at 50 percent capacity.

Up to this point in my career, I had not given any thought to where this was all going. I went to Yuk Yuk's and became a comedian. *Merv Griffin* and *Mike Douglas* were just dropped into my lap. *St. Elsewhere* came out of the blue. When I was just guest hosting for Regis, Paramount built a talk show around me. There was always something new coming my way.

But now for the first time in my career, things were being

peeled away. *St. Elsewhere* was no longer there. *Bobby's World* was finished. My TV appearances were dwindling. The talk show was canceled. My career had become traveling the country playing small theaters to even smaller crowds. This was scary. Where was I headed?

The next five years became a blur of Indian casinos, state fairs, and fund-raisers. The only constant was Las Vegas. I was still making a lot of money, but I was working twice as hard. I felt as if it were going nowhere. Jay Leno and Michael Gelman at *Regis and Kathie Lee* provided me with my only bright spots creatively. I loved and still love filling in for Regis, and Jay allowed me to come on *The Tonight Show* countless times to air my hidden camera pieces at the top of the show.

At one point, I was offered a tiny indie movie directed by Garry Marshall's son, Scott. In this movie I played a really bad guy. I looked in the mirror and thought, I don't look like a bad guy. Once again, impulse took over. I shaved my head. In my mind, the bald guy is the bad guy—except for Uncle Fester, Kojak, and Yul Brynner in *The King and I*.

I've got to tell you, it was so much fun. I went into my bathroom. I shaved just the top, and for five minutes I was Larry from the Three Stooges. Then I shaved up above my ears and became Princess Leia for the next two minutes. I then shaved it clean, got in my car, and went to the set.

When I came home from work that night, I walked into the house. Terry had not seen my head, nor did she know I had shaved it. After twenty years of marriage, what would she say? How would she react? She stepped around the corner, saw me, and was immediately taken aback.

"Oh . . . my . . . God," she said. Where is this going? I thought. After a long beat, she continued, "That is so sexy."

My knee-jerk reaction was "Wow." For her to have that reaction was wonderful. What man does not want to be considered sexy? Then the neurotic side of me kicked in. I had been with this woman for two decades. If I'm sexy now, what have I been for the last twenty years?

My initial intention was to grow my hair right back after the week's work. But it felt really clean, which is a nice thing for somebody who has issues with germs. As a shower aficionado, I believe the hair is the leading indicator. If you happen to touch your hair and it's a little oily, you will probably want to take a shower regardless of how clean you are. Of course, with my OCD just being conscious is my indicator. I looked at it as if I had just grown my face. For me, more to soap is more to enjoy.

I had been on television and in front of the public for the last twenty years, but after a few strokes of the razor, I had disappeared. No one recognized me. I could walk into a neighborhood establishment I had frequented every day and not even be acknowledged. Once I opened my mouth, they would recognize my voice. This was usually followed by a very concerned look.

"How are you?" they would ask.

"I'm fine," I'd say.

They would repeat, "Really, how are you?"

I didn't get it at first, but then it dawned on me. They thought I was ill and going through chemotherapy. My days were filled with assuring the few people who recognized me that I was fine. I could tell that they would walk away unconvinced. This is the reason I decided to grow a lip bang, or soul patch. If I have facial hair, I must be healthy.

My new look not only felt good psychologically, it enhanced my anonymity for my hidden camera pieces. It also gave me another ten minutes in my stand-up act. However, my new look and cleaner feeling were not enough to snap me out of the malaise caused by my dwindling career.

I decided to sit down and write a script for a TV pilot based on my life. The concept was a comedian with a wife and three children who happens to do hidden camera pieces for a living. The humor would come out of the fact that he would be working within a five-mile radius of his home and the effect this would have on his family.

Now, remember that I suffer from severe adult ADHD. When I say I sat down and wrote, I mean I wrote a two-line synopsis for the show. You may not believe me because you're more than 195 pages into this book. But I could never do more than a couple of pages a day, and even that was torture.

In 2004, I sold the idea to NBC. We shot a pilot entitled *Hidden Howie* that just didn't work out. I ended up doing six episodes of the show for Bravo. Professionally and psychologically, I really needed this work. This character was me, and this story was my life. I put all my energy into promoting the new show. I called in every favor I could. I made every possible TV appearance, did every piece of press you could think of, and both Jay Leno and Michael Gelman were incredibly generous in allowing me to promote the show. In spite of all my efforts, the show failed immediately.

I was so distraught that I wanted to quit the business. I was a broken man. Okay, I realize now as I write this how it must sound. People come back broken from war-torn countries or natural disasters. These are real-life catastrophes. Why was I broken? Because two networks didn't pick up my pilot. But in that moment, it was horrible. I felt I just couldn't go on in this business.

I was seriously considering other options. I had been dabbling in real estate and making investments throughout my career. I was thinking of getting involved in this full-time. Unlike show business, real estate is a profession you don't put your heart into, only your cash. If for some reason it gets taken away from you, all you've lost is your money, not your soul.

For the first time in my life, I took my destiny into my own hands. Up until now, my career was just a sequence of opportunities that had presented themselves. All of those opportunities seemed to have vanished, so I was forced to create my own. I made a conscious decision to turn away from show business and go into business without the show.

Within minutes of charting my new path, the phone rang. It was Michael Rotenberg. He told me that Endemol and NBC had called and asked if I would be interested in hosting a game show. He didn't even get the word *show* out of his mouth before I abruptly said no and hung up.

How bad could it get? I had just made a decision to leave show business. Even if I were to remain in the business, I could not imagine being a game-show host. I'm an actor. I'm a comedian. Being a game-show host would certainly be the final nail in the coffin of my career.

About fifteen minutes later, Michael called back. "Have you calmed down?" he asked.

"Yes."

"Can I just tell you a little bit about the show?"

To humor him—and maybe me—I said, "Go ahead, Michael. Tell me a little bit about the show."

"This show airs in sixty-five countries," he said. "It's a huge hit all over Europe. In fact, the host in Italy got offered millions of dollars to walk off the show by a rival network because it was cutting into their ratings."

"For a game show?" I laughed. "That's crazy."

"Let me describe the show to you," he said. "It's called *Deal or No Deal*. There are twenty-six cases. They have bikini models holding the cases, and people try to pick the case with the million dollars in it."

"Wait a second," I interrupted. "So you are telling me . . . how long is this show?"

"It's an hour," Michael said. "And NBC has devoted an entire week in prime time to launch it in December."

"What?" I asked. I thought he had just told me that NBC was going to devote an entire week of its prized prime-time schedule to launch a game show with bikini models holding briefcases.

"They are going to put it on Monday, Tuesday, Wednesday, Thursday, and Friday in the evening," he said.

"I know how many days there are in a week, and I know how television works," I shot back. "Can I just say something? The bikini models may get you thirty seconds of fun television. It sounds more like a magazine. Is there any trivia?"

"No."

"Are there any stunts?"

"No."

"Is there any skill involved?"

"No."

"Goodbye, Michael."

Five minutes later, the phone rang. Michael again. He wouldn't let this go. He told me that they really wanted me as host and that Rob Smith from Endemol would like to meet with me in person as soon as possible and pitch me the idea. I told Michael that I was going to Jerry's Deli in the Valley for lunch and if Rob wanted to buy my soup, I would listen to him.

A half hour later, I was sitting in Jerry's Deli, and a man I now know was Rob Smith walked up to my table. He introduced himself and told me that he just wanted to show me the game before I passed.

Remember, I had been told it's the biggest game in the world. Not only is it the biggest game in the world, but NBC is devoting five hours in one week of prime time to it. Endemol, I knew, did *Big Brother* and *Extreme Makeover: Home Edition*. So I sat back, ready for an elaborate song-and-dance presentation.

From under his arm, Rob pulled out an art board. In the other hand, he had a little plastic bag. I moved my soup to the left so he could put his art board on the table. I looked at the board. With a Magic Marker, he had sectioned off the board into twenty-six squares. Then he opened the plastic bag. He had made little squares with pictures of a briefcase on each one. On the other side of the squares, he had taped little pieces of paper with dollar amounts ranging from $1 to $1 million. Rob shuffled the twenty-six squares and placed them on the board. It looked like a project created by a seven-year-old with special needs.

At this point, I thought somebody was doing a hidden camera prank on me. This show was supposedly a major worldwide hit that NBC was going to air for a week in its most valuable real estate. They couldn't spend six bucks at Kinko's for a presentation? I sat and waited for the punch line.

Rob took me through the game. He told me to pick a case and not look at it. I removed one of the handmade cards and set it next to my soup. "That's your case," he said. "Now we are going to start the game. Pick six cases." I complied. He then turned them over. I saw the numbers written on them: $500, $1,000, $50,000, $25,000, $75,000, $250,000. "Right now, if I offered you a hundred and thirty thousand dollars to quit, would you take it . . . or would you keep playing and go for the million?"

"I get it," I said. "So why me?"

He talked about seeing my talk show, watching me on *St. Elsewhere,* and attending my live shows. The public's awareness of me had also just peaked because of all the press I had done for my sitcom, *Hidden Howie.* "We want somebody who has acting, comedic, and improvisational skills," he said. "You are perfect for this."

I was incredibly flattered. "If I say yes, when do I start?" I asked.

"Monday," he replied.

"Don't you have to build a set?" I asked.

"It's built."

"Don't you need twenty-six models?"

"They're cast," he said. "We are ready to shoot."

These are the moments where you realize you are not number one on the list. When they come to you just two days before production begins, you can be sure that their first, second, and third host choices must've said no. That was why I was perfect for this.

I still didn't think I wanted to do it. I went home and told Terry about the offer. Without skipping a beat, she said, "Take the deal, you idiot."

"But it's a game show," I said. "It will screw up my career."

Terry, whom I love for her beauty, her intelligence, and most of all her honesty, answered me. "What career?" she said. "You don't have a show. You want to quit the business. Why not try something new? You have nothing else to do." She's always there with her words of encouragement.

Deal or No Deal was shot at Television City, where *American Idol* and *Dancing with the Stars* are also taped. I showed up for work on my first day and was introduced to a man named Dick, who'd invented the game. He was a very sweet mathematician with a Dutch accent. He explained to me that the entire game was based on a probability equation. Dick and I were taken to a basement at the studio so he could teach me how to play.

He wanted me to be so familiar with the game board that I would focus only on the contestants. And he believed we would achieve this by making me play the game with him in a windowless room thousands of times.

Dick put the twenty-six cards in front of me and told me to talk to him as though I were hosting the game. I told him to pick a case. He did. I then told him he had four more cases to open. Dick picked $500,000. I said to him, "You just opened a big number."

Immediately, he interrupted, "Not number. Amount. Don't say 'number.' Say 'amount.' " Apparently, this was very important . . . to Dick.

Hours went by and I felt as if I were being tortured. I was holed up in a basement, being subjected to mathematical hell. I was no longer allowed to say "number"; I had to say "amount." During one break, I called Terry at home and told her that this was all her fault. I was about to snap.

They took me upstairs to the set. It was beautiful, and all the girls were, too. I began introducing myself to the models. I went up to the first girl and said, "Hi, I'm Howie. I'm the host." She turned to me and said, "You're friends with my dad." Now I felt like the old guy who was not allowed to say "number." Remember, Howie, "amount." *Amount.*

That weekend, I called some writers from *The Howie Mandel Show* to help me prepare. I thought if nothing else, I should try to be somewhat entertaining. More than anything, I was afraid of being embarrassed on national television.

Then came Monday. I was downstairs getting ready, and there was a big discussion about whether I would wear a tie and take out my earrings. They wanted me to look like a game-show host. I was fine with the tie, but I told them that I wasn't going to remove my earrings. A big negotiation ensued. I figured this would be my out. When they informed me that my earrings had been cleared by the studio brass, I was a little disappointed. I was hoping I could get out of what I believed was going to be a big embarrassing mess. It just didn't seem to me that you could fill an hour of television by pointing at cases and making offers.

The audience began pouring into the studio. The lights came up, the crowd roared, and the countdown from the control room began. I started out alone in the vault offstage. America didn't know what this show was, so they gave me these very dramatic lines to explain how it worked. I would recite these lines as I made my way to the main stage.

"Five, four, three, two, one. . . ." The show began.

"Around me are twenty-six cases," I said. "Each of these cases is holding an amount of money. One of these cases is holding one million dollars, and tonight, without any skill, without any stunts, without any trivia, somebody could walk out of here with one million dollars." As I came through the tunnel onto the main stage, I continued: "And all they have to do is answer one question." Then I walked into the light at center stage in front of the audience and asked for the first time, "Deal . . . or no deal?"

The crowd erupted on cue. I thought, Oh, my God, this is different from being in the deli with Rob from Endemol or in the basement with Dick the mathematician. This is kind of exciting. But how are we going to fill this hour?

I introduced the first contestant. I'll never forget her name: Karen Van. She jumped up out of the audience onto the stage. I was standing two feet from her. I looked into Karen's eyes and realized that this was real. We were no longer pretending. This person had hopes and dreams and a family, and if things went well, her life could be changed forever.

It hit me like a ton of bricks. At that moment, every concern I had fell by the wayside. In that split second, I was no longer a comedian hosting a game show. I didn't care about being funny. I didn't care about being entertaining. I didn't care about being embarrassed. My entire focus became about making sure that I didn't stand in the way of Karen Van walking out of there with as much money as possible.

The contestants find themselves in the center of twelve cameras, 350 people, and glaring lights. I would notice a glaze set over them. I wanted to make sure that everything was incredibly clear to them so that they could make the best decision possible. With some of the contestants, even my cadence changed. I would repeat the dollar amount over and over very slowly, making sure that it sank in.

I can't tell you how great it feels to witness somebody walking out with enough money to pay for college or buy a new house. That being said, I can't tell you how devastated I feel when a contestant walks away with nothing. I can carry that with me the entire day. I feel terrible and wonder whether I influenced their decision in any way.

The first five episodes were a tremendous experience, but I still had no concept of what I had done. I didn't know how viewers would respond. How did I know that I was not going to be the laughingstock of show business?

The shows were set to air over the Christmas vacation. As luck would have it, I had booked a family vacation on a cruise to South America. I thought it would be great for me to be out of the country and away from potential humiliation. This would be my last bastion of mental relaxation, which, by the way, I've never had in my life. I remember lying on the deck of the ship someplace in the Caribbean at the exact same time I knew the show was airing, hoping I could just stay there forever.

I woke up the next morning to an email that read, "Wow!" As it turned out, the show had set a record for NBC on a Monday, excluding football or the Olympics. The next morning, I got another email. The ratings had gone up for the second night, again breaking a record. Each day that week we got more and more viewers, and I was part of the biggest success in my professional life.

The game I initially believed was silly and the job that I had turned down were now becoming my biggest success. I don't know if my wife was more excited about the success or the fact that she could say "I told you so" for the rest of our lives. I know that had I been left to my own devices, I would not be part of it.

Just after New Year's, the ship returned to the port of Miami. As I made my way through the terminal, it began. People would recognize me and shout out, "Deal!"

The next few months were like a whirlwind. The show had

been picked up and returned to the air right after the Olympics. *Deal or No Deal* became part of the zeitgeist. There were parodies on *Saturday Night Live*, references in magazines and comic strips, and even a look-alike puppet on *Sesame Street* that plays Meal or No Meal. My own notoriety shot through the roof.

People seemed to be fascinated with my new look. I had shaved my head seven years earlier without anybody noticing. Now all of a sudden, I had created a new look for my new show.

I believe that Scott St. John, the executive producer, is the mastermind behind the success of *Deal or No Deal*. From choosing the contestants and the look of the set to the feel during game play, he built an amazing machine. All that was left for me to do was show up and allow the contestant to play the game.

For twenty-five years, I worked incredibly hard to garner attention for my humor in stand-up, my acting on television and in film, my creativity in voices on Saturday morning television. Here's what amazes me: The one place where I didn't have to perform and could just be myself becomes the biggest success in my life.

Up until this show, I had never been recognized or received an award for anything. I now have a star on the Hollywood Walk of Fame. I'm also being inducted into Canada's Walk of Fame. I have two Emmy nominations. But my greatest honor was bestowed by the waxing goddess Niki Mamakos, an aesthetician and waxing specialist in Westlake Village, California, when she added "the Howie Mandel" to her menu.

Women getting waxed now have a choice between a bikini, a Brazilian, or a Howie Mandel (just a little triangle left!). Ladies, that little shape that you see below my lip can also be above yours. It was a huge thrill, but then I got to thinking. I have a nineteen-year-old son who is dating, and if he should be lucky enough to disrobe somebody, that is the last place he wants to see any resemblance to his dad. That is definitely a no deal.

The show has not only brought me accolades, it has opened up other opportunities for me. NBC allowed me my own hidden camera show, *Howie Do It,* which was a dream come true. Allen Funt sparked my creativity with *Candid Camera* almost fifty years ago. Though I had been doing it all my life, I was now given a real platform to become my own Allen Funt. I also truly believe that without *Deal or No Deal,* you would not be reading this book.

As I write, I have already recorded over three hundred episodes of *Deal,* including prime time and syndication. I also hosted a Canadian version of *Deal.* I can't tell you how sweet success is, especially at this time in my life.

There is also a quirky aspect to this kind of recognition. People feel they can say anything to someone just because he's on TV. Ninety-nine percent of my encounters with strangers are positive, but I am truly fascinated by that other 1 percent. On any given day, somebody will walk up to me to let me know I look fatter or shorter in person. They will tell me they don't like the shaved head and that I looked so much better with hair.

I don't understand this phenomenon. I've been told they

feel comfortable telling me these things because I'm in their living room on TV every day. This makes no sense to me. My wife is in my living room every day. I would definitely not tell her that she looks a little fatter or I don't like her hair.

Deal or No Deal is everywhere. There are lottery tickets, billboards in Times Square, and people playing the handheld games. I've just recently become a bobblehead.

Last spring, I was playing the MGM Grand in Las Vegas. My wife and I were there with another couple, Louie and Kathy. They went to play the slot machines, and I went to the room. I don't know what I was doing, but it probably involved showering or washing. After a short time, I received a frantic call from my wife. "Howie, you have to get down here!" she screamed.

"What's going on?" I asked.

"Kathy just hit the jackpot!" In the background, I could hear screaming and the ringing of bells and chimes.

She told me where she was in the casino. I quickly got dressed, took the elevator down, and ran across the casino floor. As I got closer, I realized a crowd was forming around one particular machine. I made my way through to find my wife, Louie, and Kathy. The casino rep was in the midst of paying them $7,000 worth of chips. As I hugged my wife and celebrated with Louie and Kathy, I looked over at the machine that had paid out. It was a *Deal or No Deal* slot machine.

At the same time, I noticed flashbulbs coming from behind me. I turned around to see what it was. Hundreds of people had gathered and were taking pictures of me. I felt as though I were on the red carpet in front of the paparazzi.

They had no idea that I was friends with Louie and Kathy and that Terry was my wife. The crowd had originally rushed over to see what the payout was. Then it dawned on me: In their minds, when someone hit the jackpot of *Deal or No Deal*, Howie Mandel showed up personally to congratulate the winner.

I addressed everyone: "Thank you for coming. I must be off. Someone just hit the jackpot in Reno." And I ran off to find the next winner. When it comes to *Deal or No Deal*, I feel as if I'm the winner.

GOODBYE

It was May 21, 2009, my lowest point physically. I couldn't breathe. I felt like shit. And I couldn't even make it up the stairs to my bedroom.

I was going to the hospital to have my ablation. I was trying to focus on how lucky I was to have a flutter. The flutter was on the right side of my heart. The flutter caused all the other problems. If the doctor could just burn away the flutter, then I would be fixed. I don't know how to describe this excitement. Let's just say I was all a-flutter. For those of you who don't remember, Dr. Cannom told me they had to burn the right side of my heart, which made the procedure a lot less complicated than if it were on the left side.

I was having it done at Good Samaritan Hospital in downtown L.A. I arrived, checked in, and put on my standard-issue hospital gown. A young doctor came in to have me sign a release. He went over all the improbable dangers of the procedure. Apparently, these were minuscule. I could have a heart attack, a stroke, or a bad reaction to the anesthesia. In short, I could die. I had never been more scared in my life. I was consumed with the fact that I might never wake up again.

To put me at ease, he said there was only a one-in-a-thousand chance of anything going wrong. He said it as if these odds would lessen my anxiety. My mind went right back to October 1987, when fourteen thousand people came to see me at Radio City Music Hall. If fourteen of those people had dropped dead, I would've considered that a really bad night. But you have to remember, according to this doctor those were great odds, because that's still *only* one out of every thousand. So with that in mind, he asked if I would please sign the release. I fluttered. I signed.

An IV was inserted into my arm. I was quickly wheeled into the operating room. It looked like the bridge in the new *Star Trek* movie. It was very bright, with high-tech equipment enveloping a table. Five or six technicians were working on various things in the room. Everybody was incredibly pleasant. As much as I believe the chitchat was all about comforting me, it was disconcerting having to make small talk with people who were going to render me unconscious, strip me, shave me, and eventually dig into my groin and burn my heart.

Right before they put me out, I sat up while they taped a penny onto my back. I would imagine the penny was used as a marker for some sort of imaging, but I like to think of it as a good-luck thing. That's the last thing I remember.

After what seemed like a minute, I was once again awake. Dr. Cannom and Dr. Ivan Ho—how's that for literature?—were standing to my right. Let me digress for a minute. That was actually the doctor's name. What's even more exciting for me is the fact that hopefully someday at some time someone might mention reading the portion of my book that referenced Ivan Ho. Even though it's spelled somewhat differently, the fact that there is a possible reference to nineteenth-century British literature in a Howie Mandel book sets my heart a-flutter.

My first words to the doctors were "Am I done?"

To which they responded, "No."

"What do you mean, 'no'?"

"We went in the right side and zapped your flutter, but apparently that was not your problem," Dr. Cannom explained. "The main problem is on your left side."

My mind began to race. The good news about the flutter was that it was on the right side, the less complicated side. Now they had to work on the left side, where there was a higher probability of audience members dying.

I became defiant. "I'm not coming back," I said. "I'm not doing this again." I don't know what I was thinking. I'll show them. I'll just sit at home, unable to breathe. Boy, will they feel bad.

Apparently, while I was still out, Dr. Cannom had told Terry that the procedure hadn't worked and he had an opening on May 26 to bring me back and do the more involved procedure. I didn't know this, but she broke down and cried. She had been under a lot of stress over the last few months, watching as I suffered.

May 26 also happens to be Terry's birthday. I can think of better ways to celebrate than . . . I'm going to be totally honest. I was going to try to come up with something really funny here, but my mind is so fucked up that I can't.

The next five days were hell. My heart rate was becoming more and more erratic. My breathing was more stilted. My fear of the more elaborate procedure was magnified by the fact that I had gone through it before. As someone whose whole being is about maintaining control and avoiding germs, there seemed to be no more out-of-control feeling than being knocked unconscious, shaved, cut, and handled by strangers.

I couldn't stop shaking.

May 26, 2009. I woke up and wished Terry a happy birthday. Off to the hospital we went.

I was told the procedure would take three to four hours. I drove the doctors crazy with questions about how this would be different from the first time. They told me that the only difference was that I would wake up with a catheter.

"No!" I screamed. As a kid, I hated crazy straws. I certainly didn't want one inserted into my penis.

He tried to calm me. "It's really very simple," he said. "The nurse will come in and pull it out in the morning."

"It's very simple for you," I said. "I don't want anything in my penis, or anything pulled out of my penis."

He explained to me that they fill me with so much liquid, it must be drained. I told him that I would take care of it. Just make sure the catheter is out before I see it.

Ten hours. That's how long the procedure took. Apparently, this was no flutter, but it was done. I was so excited. Drs. Cannom and Ivan Ho were like my genies in a bottle. They granted me my three wishes. Number one was that I would survive. I'm writing this now, so obviously it was a wish come true. Number two, I would be able to breathe. I'm inhaling and exhaling like a pervert making obscene phone calls. And number three, let me check. I'm slowly lifting my gown and revealing my bruised and taped groin. Yes, no catheter! All three wishes had been granted. Do you believe in magic? I do.

There was a price to not having the catheter. I had been injected with twelve pounds of fluid during the procedure. I was barely lucid after ten hours of anesthesia. I would wake up every few minutes to drain myself into a container. I was incredibly thirsty, so they had also given me a container of apple juice. I think you can see where this is going. I don't need to relive it.

The next morning, another doctor came into my room, said hello, and without further ado ripped the tape from my crotch and was gone before I could say, "And your name is . . ."

I pulled the blankets up over me and began to drink more apple juice. I assume it was apple juice. As I was drinking, my groin began to feel moist. Was this shit going right through me? I had the eerie feeling that I was pissing myself. Was there a ditch or a puddle nearby? This was so embarrassing. I didn't want to call a nurse. In fact, I didn't want to call anybody. I gingerly lifted the blanket to inspect, and lo and behold, with every beat of my heart, blood was pulsating out of the wound. I was about to pass out at the sight, so I let out a bloodcurdling scream: "Help!"

The doctor who'd just taken the tape off ran back into the room and asked what the problem was. I showed him. He said, "Oh, that's nothing to worry about." This is something I want to pass on to my readers: If you should ever wake up with blood streaming out of your groin, apparently it's nothing to worry about.

"I just have to apply pressure for ten minutes," he said. He put on two latex gloves, placed one hand on top of the other, and pressed with all his weight on my groin. You have to remember, I'm a guy who doesn't enjoy personal contact with strangers. It probably would've been more comfortable for me just to shake this gentleman's hand rather than have him face-to-face with me, leaning over and doing push-ups off my groin. We were literally nose to nose, making stilted, awkward, uncomfortable chitchat. After ten minutes of psychological hell, the floodgates were closed. And the tiny village of groin was safe once again.

I was released from the hospital and went home to resume my life. The strange coincidence was that as I set out to write this book, I was diagnosed with afib, a physical condition. The bad news was that I was sure I was at death's door. The good news was that this would become a runaway bestseller because I had prophesied my own death and the book had to be put together posthumously.

Nothing has changed mentally since I had the ablation. My life is filled with the torture of OCD, adult ADHD, and assorted other acronyms for mental issues. I still think there is a pretty good possibility I will die before I end this paragraph. It's months before the book comes out, and I don't know if I'll be here while you are reading this.

There's so much that I haven't included in this book. I was just saying the other day how I have enough material for another book. In no way should the brass at Bantam Dell see this as a negotiating ploy. Looking back at what I did include, I'm haunted. I'm embarrassed. I'm excited. I'm embarrassed. I can't believe I actually finished a book. I'm worried that I might have offended somebody. But most of all, I'm embarrassed. If you approach me with this book, I may have a hard time making eye contact because you now know the truth about me.

Let's recap. I started out a lactose-intolerant, urinating outcast who fell into ditches and puddles, sometimes walked like Quasimodo, had a fear of laundry hampers, was a nesting ground for sand flies, and craved 100 percent of the attention. I then became a color-blind carpet salesman who did stand-up comedy. I went on to become a television and movie actor, recording artist, voice-over talent, Saturday morning cartoon, decoy, daytime talk show host, and game-show host. Since I have become so public with my issues, I have done a public service announcement for OCD, testified on Capitol Hill about mental health issues, and become the poster boy for

Adult ADHD Is Real (adultadhdisreal.com). I guess you can call me a mental spokesmodel—and now an author. I can't wait to find out what's next. Most important, I am a son, a brother, a husband, a father, and a friend. I guess what I'm trying to say to my mother, my brother, my wife, my children, and all my friends and co-workers is, I don't know how you put up with me. So, sorry, but hey, we got a book out of it.

So things are good, and for you, the reader, I have one final thought I can't express enough. Here's the deal: Don't touch me.

P.S. I had to put this in. I just received a call to go to Starbucks, where a group of Chabad rabbis are going to present me with a basketball. I don't know if I should've told you this now or saved it for the opening of my next book.

ACKNOWLEDGMENTS

I would like to acknowledge:

The loves of my life: my wife, Terry, my children, Jackie, Alex, and Riley, my parents, Al and Evy, and my brother, Steve, for loving me and supporting me, but mostly for putting up with me.

Michael Rotenberg, my friend, my manager, and my second brother, who has been on this journey with me from the beginning.

Rich Thurber, my road manager, who has also become part of my family.

Andy Cohen and Steve Levine, friends and agents, the procurers of the jobs that provided many of the stories.

Bill Sobel, my attorney and friend, for making sure I have always been treated fairly.

John Mendoza, my friend and fellow comedian, for hanging with me on the road and listening to me talk about myself for countless hours while putting this book together.

Josh Young, my co-writer and new friend, for helping me put my life in readable form and maintain focus for more than ten minutes at a time.

Philip Rappaport, my editor, for his input and editorial guidance.

Nita Taublib and her team at Bantam Dell for their efforts in bringing the book to market.

Andrea Barzvi, my literary agent, for pushing to make it happen.

Lewis Kay and Nicki Fioravante, my publicists, for coordinating the promotion of this book.

All the people who have hired me in the past and given me phenomenal opportunities to shine, such as the always supportive Michael Gelman and the brilliant Scott St. John, the executive producer of *Deal or No Deal*, because without the success of that show I doubt I would've ever been asked to write a book.